THE BEAU ENGLISHMAN

The Life, Loves & Travels of a Georgian Socialite:
Rev Dr Thomas Sedgwick Whalley

CHRIS STEPHENS

Bristol Books CIC, The Courtyard, Wraxall,
Wraxall Hill, Bristol, BS48 1NA

The Beautiful Englishman,
written and researched by Chris Stephens

Published by Bristol Books 2020

ISBN: 9781909446212

Copyright: Chris Stephens

Design: Joe Burt

A CIP record for this book is available from the British Library.

ABOUT THE AUTHOR

When he retired from academic dentistry in 2002, Chris Stephens was able to spend more time undertaking charitable work for the Woodland Trust and the Dry Stone Walling Association, of which he had been Deputy Chairman. His interest in local history arose thorough helping to rebuild the dry stone walls of the Trust's Dolebury Warren Wood.

Chris is an emeritus Professor of the University of Bristol and received an OBE for his services to dental education in 1999. He is an Honorary Life Member of both the British and European Orthodontic Societies, a Fellow of the British Dental Association and is currently Vice President of the Dry Stone Walling Association of Great Britain.

Chris, centre, talking to HRH The Prince of Wales, Patron of the Dry Stone Walling Association of Great Britain.

ACKNOWLEDGEMENTS

Many people have been of great assistance in the collection of material for this book. First I must thank the members of the Langford History Group, particularly Alex Kolombos, John Gowar, Jo Fryer, Stan Croker and Pat Wilson, for their help and encouragement. Then there was Sheila Johnson, of the Blagdon History Society, who provided me with many pieces of information about North Somerset, and Maria Forbes, who was my source of knowledge about the history of Winscombe. Dr Moira Bonnington, a national authority on the 'Macaronis', gave me great assistance in unravelling the histories of General Horneck, the Military Macaroni, and his first wife, later to become Mrs Horneck Whalley, while Kathryn Byrnell's diligent research led to the discovery of who the mysterious Reverend Robert Boyle (O')Sullivan really was.

Contact with members of the Chippenham/La Flèche Twinning Group on both sides of the Channel, and in particular Richard and Karin Meek in England and Monique and Guy Massé in France, led to the publication of a short article in *Cahier Fléchois* and the discovery of the house in La Fléche which Thomas Whalley bought for his niece, Frances. The documents detailing its purchase and later sale were then translated by my good friend Kevin Byrne.

Finally I am most grateful to the staff who assisted me in accessing the records held in both the Somerset and Bristol Archives.

Mendip Lodge as it was in 2005 (Map reference ST 467591).

INTRODUCTION

I FIRST DISCOVERED the ruins of Mendip Lodge in 2005 while working as a volunteer for the Woodland Trust in the adjacent Dolebury Warren Wood, above Upper Langford in North Somerset. I then spent the next 10 years researching the life of its remarkable builder and owner.

The personable Reverend Dr Thomas Sedgwick Whalley DD (1746-1827) was able to lead an affluent life through his marriages to two wealthy women. He acquired a wide circle of influential literary friends through the lavish entertainment he provided, both at 20, Royal Crescent, Bath, and at his country residence, Langford Court, in North Somerset. While he was to have no children of his own, the death of his beloved sister brought the responsibility of bringing up his nine-year-old niece Frances, a highly talented but headstrong girl who was to cause him both joy and pain over the next 50 years.

After his disastrous third marriage, Thomas separated from his wife and, in declining health, decided to move to Bristol to be closer to his friend, Mrs Piozzi (Mrs Hester Lynch Thrale), and his relative, Penelope Weston, now the wife of William Pennington, Master of the Ceremonies at the Hotwell. Yet this was not to be and, having transferred the lease of 4, Windsor Terrace, to Hannah More, he died in France after rescuing his much-loved niece from penury.

EARLY LIFE

W HEN PROFESSOR THE Reverend John Whalley died in 1748, his widow moved her family from Cambridge back to Wells where her father, the Reverend Francis Squire, was Chancellor of the Cathedral. Through his good offices she was able to move into the Tower House, which was only a few yards from his own and still stands close to the north porch of the Cathedral.

Very little is known of the early life of the family. The eldest son, John, had attended Charterhouse School and then Cambridge before entering the Welsh Fusiliers, but died only a few years later on the homeward passage from India at the age of 26 years. John's younger brother, Francis, seems then to have become the nominal head of the household at the age of 21. Of Mrs Whalley's three daughters, her eldest married a doctor and takes no further part in this story; her next daughter, Mary, married James Wickham, an attorney of Frome, in the year that her eldest brother John had died. They play a minor role.

But our story really concerns Thomas, who was still at school at this time, and his sister, Elizabeth, who was one year his senior. He adored her and later commissioned at least two paintings of her, one of which he kept with him all his life.

Thomas Sedgwick Whalley in 1781, aged 35 years, with Sappho. This is an engraving by Joseph Brown (1809-1887), made from the painting by Joshua Reynolds, the whereabouts of which is unknown. It seems almost certain that Hill Wickham arranged for the engraving to be made so it could be included in his book which was published in 1863.

Elizabeth Sage née Whalley. Another engraving by Joseph Brown of a painting by George Romney (1704-1842).

According to his nephew, Hill Wickham, who wrote what is a biography of his uncle in all but name, Thomas maintained that neither did her beauty justice.[1]

No early correspondence between Thomas and his sister survives but she is described by his nephew as being possessed of remarkable personal attractions, a sweet and affectionate disposition and a cultivated understanding, but was of a delicate disposition. Such a description is certainly borne out by later correspondence and events.

Thomas was likely to have been first educated by his mother and sisters but later by a Mr Davis of Ilminster.[2, 3] This was probably at the Ilminster Free School, which had been established in 1440, the same year in which Henry VI founded

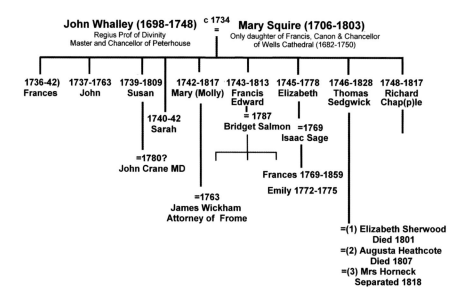

The Whalley family tree.

Eton College and several other free schools.[4] The Annals Cantab has a cryptic entry for a Thomas Davis of '*Perhaps V(icar). of Ilminster, Somerset, till 1768*'. Thomas entered St. John's Cambridge at 18 years of age in April, 1763, and matriculated in Michaelmas the same year, which would indicate that his earlier schooling had been well spent. It is curious that he did not enter Peterhouse Hall, where his father had been Professor and Vice Chancellor, particularly when the college had a tradition of encouraging poetry, which was to prove to be a lifelong passion for Thomas. It is perhaps relevant to his choice of St. John's that the college had the best library at the time,[5] but more importantly his cousin, Richard Beadon, was a fellow and a tutor there and about to become the Orator for the University. The two were to remain close friends in later life, during which time Beadon would become Bishop of Gloucester and then Bishop of Bath and Wells. In June, 1789, as the new Bishop of Gloucester, he wrote to Thomas:

My Dear Sir,

I lose no time in acknowledging the favour of your letter and requesting your acceptance of my best thanks for your kind congratulations and good wishes on my late promotion...

...You are not within my diocese but so near the borders of it, that I am not without hopes of you having some time or other to call towards Gloucester, so as to make a visit to the palace as little inconvenient to you, as it would be highly gratifying to myself and Mrs Beadon....

Thomas was clearly both able and diligent in his scholarship. He is reported as having retained till his latest days the custom of rising early and reading scripture, either in the septuagint version (an ancient Greek translation of the Old Testament) or in the Greek new testament. He was well acquainted with the French and Italian languages. The latter was not surprising since, until 1792, degree examinations in Cambridge were conducted orally and in Latin! In later life Thomas was virtually bilingual in French, though we are told with a very poor accent.

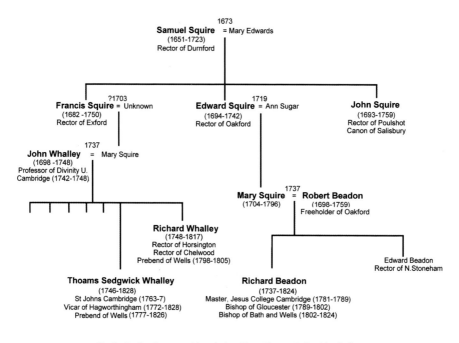

The Squire family tree and its relationship to Thomas Sedgwick Whalley.

Obtaining his degree in 1767, Thomas did not take holy orders for another three years. Almost certainly this time was spent on a Grand Tour which was very fashionable at that time for anyone with the wherewithal to do so. This would also account for his excellent French, his later architectural taste, and several lifelong continental friends with whom he maintained a correspondence for more than 50 years. It seems doubtful though whether his tour extended into Italy, as the correspondence between him and his brother, Francis, when the latter was in Rome, does not suggest that Thomas had any previous knowledge of life in Italy.[6]

While he was away, his beautiful elder sister, the 24-year-old Elizabeth, had married Isaac Sage (1741-1818), who was the third youngest of nine children of John Sage and Elizabeth Sage, of Stanmore in Middlesex.[7] In 1762 Isaac, or more likely his wealthy father, had petitioned the East India Company in London for his admission into its service as a writer.[8] This was the usual route of entry to the company but was no simple matter. Although "John Company" recruited a dozen men to enter its service each year, this was undertaken by competition, for which there was an entry fee payable, equivalent to £50,000 today.[9] Such applications were normally made at age 16 years, so the 21-years-old Isaac was slightly older than average, but this was by no means unusual. Robert, later Major-General Lord Clive of Plassey, was 19-years-old when his father acquired a similar position for him in 1744.

According to Hill Wickham, Isaac eventually became paymaster to Robert Clive's Indian army before his return to England,[10] but this seems doubtful. However, Isaac had certainly returned from India a rich man, probably in 1767 when many senior servants of the company in Bengal were either dismissed or resigned.[11] Quite what size fortune he had amassed during his five years in India can only be guessed at. General Smith, a friend who returned in 1770, did so with a fortune believed to be equivalent to £20-£30m today.[12] However, Smith had spent three times as long as Isaac in the company's service.

On his return from India, Isaac probably lodged first with his parents before buying a house in London and renting a house for the season in Bath, with the intention of finding a wife.[13] Two years later, in May, 1769, Elizabeth Whalley and Isaac were married in the Whalley's family church of St Cuthbert's, Wells. Their daughter, Frances, was born four months later, though Hill Wickham, in his account written almost 100 years later, states that the marriage had taken place in 1768. However the parish records are quite clear on the matter. One must assume that the pre-dating of the marriage was to avoid offending Victorian sensibilities,[14] though in the mid 18th century almost half the brides went to the altar pregnant.

After their marriage, Isaac and Elizabeth lived in London. Their first address was Queen Anne Street and it is clear that they were in close contact with the Sage's at their family home at Stanmore, and also with Isaac's younger brother, Joseph, and his wife, who lived at Reading. Joseph (1758-1820) was, for 40 years, Assayer to the Royal Mint.[15]

Sometime in 1770, Thomas returned to England and met his new brother-in-law and niece. In September of the same year he was ordained deacon by Edward Wilkes, Bishop of Bath and Wells, in the Chapel of the Bishop's Palace.[16] Two years later, on 15th March, 1772, he was ordained priest by Bishop Richard Terrick in the Chapel Royal, London, and only two days

Thomas Sedgwick Whalley, aged 25 years. in a miniature by John Taylor (1739-1838).
This is dated 1771 © Trustees of the British Museum

later was presented with the living of Hagworthingham, a parish of about 300 souls in Lincolnshire. It would seem that this was in the gift of Edmund Keene, Bishop of Ely, who had held Professor John Whalley in high regard.[17] Although a graduate of Caius, Keene became a Fellow of Peterhouse and obtained his doctorate there in the time of Whalley's father.

Thomas Sedgwick's living had a singular provision from the Bishop, which was that Thomas was never to reside there since the air of the fens was fatal to anyone but a native.[18] Happy to comply, Thomas immediately hired a curate to represent him and never went there again. He was obviously grateful for this living but perhaps felt a little guilty about it. Three years before his death, he arranged for a new parsonage to be built there at his own expense and, in his Will, he bequeathed £300 to generate interest to support a Sunday school.

In June, 1773, Thomas received a letter from his brother Richard, who was now in Rome training to be an historical painter.[19] In this we learn that Thomas had *departed for Wales*. The letter was addressed to the Reverend Warrington at Little Acton, Wrexham. Both George Warrington (1744-1830) and Thomas had matriculated from St. John's Cambridge in the same year and were to remain lifelong friends. The last letter between them is dated October 30th, 1827, within a year of Thomas Sedgwick's death, in which George addresses Thomas as *My Dear Old Friend*.[20]

George had been born in Wrexham, and had married Mary Strudwick in 1768, the year after he graduated from Cambridge. She was the daughter of a wealthy Jamaican plantation owner, with estates of 1,900 acres in the West Indies. By 1773, George had been ordained and had become Cannon of St Asaph's, in whose diocese Wrexham lay. Elizabeth Sage, in a letter of August, refers to Thomas having taken a Curacy in Wales,[21] though there is no record

Holy Trinity Hagworthingham.

of him holding such an appointment. However, this was probably a local arrangement made by George Warrington or the local landowner.

In three letters to Thomas from his sister, over the summer of that year, we learn of the Sage's very full social life. The first of these, dated July, 1773, is from their London home in Queen Anne Street and is addressed, perhaps slightly mockingly, to "Dear Rev Brother". It describes days spent at the races, and visits to the homes of General Smith, Mr Batson and Mr Lutterell, all prominent East Indiamen. For much of this time Elizabeth's two daughters, Frances, aged four, and Emily aged two, were left with her parents-in-law at Stanmore.

Despite this very active social life, it appears that Elizabeth was not well. Hill Wickham records that she always had a delicate constitution and this is clear from her subsequent two letters of August.[22] In the second of these she writes to "dearest Tom" from Bristol, the Sages having travelled down from London in stages in their own phaeton. She says:

> You will see by the date of this letter that we are at the Hot Well, where I
> am very sanguine in my hopes of receiving benefit. The waters have greatly

relieved my complaints already. I have brought my dear Fanny with me, and left Emily with my mother (Mrs Whalley senior at Wells) who was to carry her over to Winscombe (where her elder brother Francis was now living)* to be there while I am here, which will be 6 weeks if the waters continue to agree with me.[23]

*Francis Edwards Whalley had purchased the lease of "The Parsonage House of Winscombe" (ie. Winscombe Court) in September 1771.

She also expresses the wish that Thomas could find time from his commitment in Wales to visit and see his two nieces:

My Fanny is so good a girl, and so very sensible, (I think I may say so impartially) that she is a very agreeable companion to me. Your god-daughter (Emily) is a sweet cherub and now runs quite alone and begins to chatter.

She adds a footnote which both indicates the keen interest Thomas had in her life as well as the frankness which existed between them.

You ask me whether I am in the way of bringing another brat [into the world], *or whether you dreamt it? Certainly, the latter.* [24]

In a later letter, dated August 21st, 1773, Elizabeth says:

I hear of your leaving Wales with pleasure; I have been somewhat jealous of their detaining you there so long already. I shall look on the hopes you give me of spending a few days with us in town, as a promise, and if you should exceed that time we shall not show you the door. A pretty gentleman you are to talk of days, when you visit a sister whom you have not seen for this, I do not know how long; it appears to me as an age, as I measure the time by my affection.[25]

In fact Thomas would not leave Wrexham for another four months. This delay seems have been brought about because George and his wife had to go London to await the arrival her late father's executor who was sailing from Jamaica in connection with the estates which George's wife had inherited.[26, 27] Thomas seems to have agreed to stay on to deputise for him.[28]

It is not clear if his sister was aware of this since, in a letter from Elizabeth dated only Autumn, 1773, (but with the added note "I have too many things to think of to remember the day of the month"), she again expresses the wish that her brother would soon return home.

> Pack up your alls and begone from Little Acton! I am sure your friends must be heartily tired of you by this. We long to be so plagued in our turn......My dear girls are quite well and as .....but come and see them, I will not give you an account of them or anything else!

More interestingly she concludes by saying:

> If you are in the widow's good graces, you should not boast of her favours; at least defer your information till we are tête à tête. In truth, I shall begin to harbour some suspicions if you stay at Acton much longer.

> The first wish of my heart is to see my dear favourite brother well settled; no one is more formed for domestic happiness, and I trust the good Bishop will, ere it is long, enable you to offer your hand and heart to some woman who is worthy of you, if among women there is such to be found. [29]

So it would seem that Thomas was already seeking a wife by this time. It is also odd that Elizabeth is unaware that her brother had been appointed Rector of Hagworthingham 19 months earlier! In a further letter, again dated Autumn, 1773, Elizabeth is now in London with her husband and reports that their mutual friends, the Warringtons, are also there (presumably having arrived to await the arrival of Mr Strudwicke's executor).[30] It is clear from this, and from the previous letter from their youngest brother, Richard, that the Warringtons by this time were close friends of all the Whalley family. Elizabeth continues:

> Pray present my compliments to the amiable widow of your [unknown] friend; I feel for her in the absence of a husband......[31]

But who is this amiable widow? Was she the same as he had met in Wrexham? Could it indeed perhaps be Mrs Sherwood, née Jones, of Langford Court who Thomas would soon marry? Her husband had been John Withers Sherwood, a barrister, who had died three years earlier. The Whalleys and the Sherwoods must have known each other since John Withers Sherwood's maternal grandfather and great grandfather had been Canons of Wells and his maternal grandfather, the Rev Thomas Eyre, had preceded Thomas' maternal grandfather as Chancellor of Wells Cathedral.

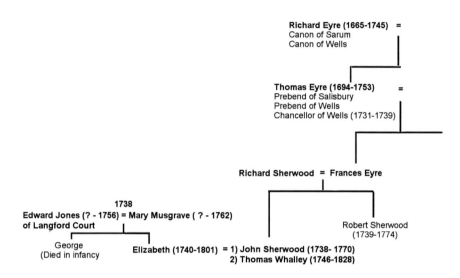

The Jones/Eyre/Sherwood family tree.

Thomas' belated return to Wells was not without incident, for en route he fell from his horse and was seriously concussed. This must have been somewhere near to Wells as he was soon confined to bed in his mother's house. His sister's next recorded letter is dated Boxing Day, 1773, and is from Lovell Hill, home of the Berkshire nabob Hugh Watts, who had been born in India but whose family came from Berkshire. He had bought the house in 1767 on his return from India and may well have travelled back on the same boat as Isaac Sage. In the Boxing Day letter, she records:

Two- and- fifty dined at the house yesterday; and the servants were as merry as their masters.[32]

She also enquires after Thomas, who is recovering in Wells, and Elizabeth hopes *"that sleeping in his own chamber, the quietude has promoted sleep and that she will observe the good consequences of it"* when she joins him there. (The footnote by Hill Wickham confirms this is following his recent fall from his horse when returning from Wales). More relevant to Thomas' pursuit of a suitable wife, Elizabeth also asks:

I hope by this you have had a good account of dear Mrs Sherwood.[33]

From this it would seem that Elizabeth was unaware that Thomas was now being nursed by Mrs Sherwood. A year later, on the first anniversary of his marriage, he describes in gushing terms how it had been her kind ministrations to him after his fall which convinced him of her merits as a wife.[34]

Thomas' recovery must have been remarkable since marriage took place only 11 days later, on January 6th, 1774, and in St Marylebone Church, Westminster! It was conducted by Bishop Edmund Keene of Ely who had provided Thomas with his living at Hagworthingham two years earlier. Others in attendance included his sister, Elizabeth, and her husband, who signed the register, as did Thomas' cousin, Dr Richard Beadon, who was now a prebend of St Pauls and would eventually become Bishop of Bath and Wells.

Thomas' marriage at St Marylebone Church, Westminster.

CHAPTER 2

MARRIAGE AND
LIFE IN BATH

M ARRIAGE BROUGHT THOMAS great wealth. Elizabeth Sherwood was the surviving child and thus heiress of Edward Jones, of Langford Court. According to his Will, Elizabeth was only to have a life interest in the family estate but it seems that her first husband, John Withers Sherwood, a lawyer, had started legal proceedings to break entail in anticipation that he would have children to inherit the Jones estate. Thomas seems to have taken advantage of this and progressed matters further. He does, though, seem to have had something of a conscience about doing so and he cannot have had any expectation of children. Not only had his wife produced no heirs for her former husband but it would seem that, in seeking a wife in Wales, Thomas had been only interested in childless widows.

When Elizabeth Sherwood and Thomas Sedgwick Whalley married on 6th January, 1774, she was aged 34 and he just 28 years. Surprisingly they were married in Marylebone, Middlesex, though neither appear to have been living in London at the time.[35] We know nothing of Mrs Sherwood's education and early life but intriguingly there was a Mrs Sherwood who, during 1768/69, was a player in the Bath/Bristol Theatre Company.[36] If this was the same person, it would fit with the suggestion that her first husband fell ill sometime in 1769, necessitating her leaving the theatre to nurse him until his death in August, 1770. While this is pure speculation there is no doubt that Elizabeth shared a passion with the would-be playwright Thomas Sedgwick. For example, when, two years after their marriage, their guests were snowed-in at Langford Court, a play had been written by Thomas which was then performed by those detained there:

One party was remembered by all present. A company of neighbours came to dinner on a winter's evening in 1776, and during their stay, which in those days was protracted, far beyond the limits of modern fashion (the author Hill Wickham was writing this in 1863), the snow fell so fast that when the carriages were ordered it was impossible to leave, and some of the more distant neighbours were detained, not unwilling prisoners for several days. For animal cheer, the sheepfold, close at hand, supplied good mutton in abundance; and the cellar, famous since the days of an old Somersetshire toast "A bumper Squire Jones!" was well calculated to keep the blood in active circulation. To prevent ennui a play was written and performed, and various pieces of poetry composed and recited.[37]

One of the poems composed by Thomas Sedgwick on this occasion, and recited by him, has been preserved.(See Appendix 1). Hill Wickham says that Miss Luders, a Bath resident and the sister of Theodore von Luders, who later would accompany the Whalleys on their continental tour, made a pen for Dr Whalley and insisted on him writing a copy for her. This was subsequently lost, but the 200 lines which Hill Wickham reproduces were recalled from memory by Mrs Torriano (née La Fausille) who had also been present.[38]

From the poem we can deduce that those present on this occasion included Mrs G Anstey, Miss La Fausille, Mary Whalley, who would marry Dr John Crane, Susan Wickham, née Whalley, and her husband, James Wickham, Mrs Knollis (this is likely to be the widow of the Reverend Charles Knollis, the 5th Earl of Banbury), Mrs Rodd, Miss Luders, and Monsieur Zenovief (was this perhaps Zinovieff?), who appears to be the Russian ambassador. One thing this tells us is that, as early as 1776, Thomas was already keenly writing poetry and already had a wide and influential circle of friends.

Quite where Thomas' interest in poetry came from is not clear.[39] However, it is likely that, while in Cambridge, he was in contact with the poets of Pembroke Hall, where Thomas Gray still held court. This would certainly account for his later immediate friendship with Wilberforce and his support for the politics of William Pitt, both of whom graduated later from Pembroke Hall. At that time the College had a tradition of encouraging the study of oratory and poetry and Wilberforce and Pitt became notable parliamentary orators.

After their marriage, Elizabeth and Thomas lived at Langford Court, where Thomas was later responsible for adding bays and a west wing to the original 17th century house.[40] However, it was clearly Whalley's intention to get closer to the social centre of Bath.

Langford Court: the west wing was added by Thomas Sedgwick Whalley.

Hill Wickham states that *'within a year or two of his marriage Thomas had bought the centre house in the Crescent at Bath'*.[41] It seems though that the Whalley's house may have been bought for her husband by Elizabeth in 1775, the year after their marriage. Lowndes, quoting Philip Gosse,[42] says that number 9 was the first house to be completed and had been bought in 1768 by Philip Thicknesse, an ambitious and ill-tempered soldier of fortune.[43] Thicknesse lived there with his third wife until 1774, whereupon he sold it to a *'lady of quality'* for £2,000. This was almost certainly the new Mrs Whalley. Ison identifies number 9, later renumbered as 20, being occupied by the Rev Thomas Sedgwick Whalley in 1778,[44] and William Lowndes is quite definite in stating that Thomas Sedgwick bought the house currently numbered 20.[45] Although by current numbering the "centre house" would be number 15 or

16, it is likely that Hill Wickham never visited the house while his great uncle owned it.

It now became the Whalleys' custom to spend only the summer months at Langford Court and the rest of the year in Bath, where they were soon being noted for their lavish literary soirées. Fanny Burney, who later became Madame D'Arblay, was already the successful novelist of '*Evelina*' when she was invited to join one of the Whalley's soirees at Royal Crescent. She described Thomas as '*immensely tall, thin and handsome, but affected delicate and sentimental(ly) pathetic*'. Her diary description of what must have been a typical gathering at Royal Crescent on 27th May, 1780, paints a very vivid picture of the occasion:

In the Afternoon we all went to the Whalleys, where we found a large & high Dressed Company:- at the Head of which sat Lady Miller. Among the rest, were Mr. Anstey, his lady & 2 Daughters, Miss Weston, Mrs Aubrey, the thin quaker like woman I saw first at Mrs Laws's - Mrs Lamber-, & various others, male & female, that I knew not.

Miss Weston (a cousin of Thomas' wife) instantly made up to me, to express her delight at my return to Bath, & to beg she might sit by me, - Mrs Whalley, however, placed me upon a sofa next herself & that meagre fright Mrs Aubrey - which, however, I did not repine at, for the extreme delicacy of Miss Weston makes it prodigiously fatiguing to converse with her, as it is no little difficulty to keep pace with her refinement in order to avoid shocking her by too obvious an inferiority in daintihood & ton.

Mr Whalley, to my great astonishment, so far broke through his delicacy, as to call to me across the Room to ask me divers questions concerning my London Journey:- during all which Mr Anstey, who sat next to him, earnestly fixed his Eyes in my Face, & both then, & for the rest of the Evening, examined me with a look of most keen penetration.

As soon as my discourse was over with Mr Whalley, during which, as he called me by my Name, every body turned towards me, - which was not very agreeable,- Lady Miller arose, & went to Mrs Thrale, & whispered something to her. Mrs Thrale then rose too, & said 'If your Ladyship will give me leave. I will first introduce my Daughter to you, - making Miss Thrale, who was next her mother, make her reverences, - 'And now, she continued, Miss Burney, Lady Miller desires to be introduced to you,' - Up I jumped, & walked forward, - Lady Miller, very civilly, more than met me half way, & said very polite things of her wish to know me, & regret that she had not sooner met me, - & then we both returned to our seats.

Do you know now that notwithstanding Bath Easton is so much Laughed at in London, nothing here is more tonish than to visit Lady Miller, who is extremely curious in her Company, admitting few people who are not of Rank or of Fame, & excluding of those all who are not people of character very unblemished.

Some Time after, Lady Miller took a seat next mine on the sofa, to play at Cards, - & was excessively civil indeed, - scolded Mrs Thrale for not sooner making us acquainted, & had the politeness to offer to take me to the Balls, herself, as she heard Mr & Mrs Thrale did not chuse to go.

After all this, it is hardly fair to tell you what I think of her, - however, the truth is I always, to the best of my intentions, speak honestly what I think of the folks I see, without being biassed either by their civilities or neglect, - & that, you will allow, is being a very faithful Historian.

Well then, - Lady Miller is a round, plump, course(sic) looking Dame of about 40, - &, while all her aim is to appear an elegant Woman of Fashion, all her success is to seem an ordinary Woman in very common Life with fine Cloaths on. Her manners are bustling, her Air is mock-important, & her Language very inelegant.

So much for the Lady of Bath Easton, - who, however, seems extremely good natured, & who is, I am sure, extremely civil.

The Card Party was soon after broken up, as Lady Miller was engaged to Lady Dorothy English, & then I moved to seat myself by Mrs Lambart. I was presently followed by Miss Weston, - & she was pursued by Mr Bouchier, a man of Fortune who is in the Army, or the militia, & who was tormenting Miss Weston, en badinage, about some expedition upon the River Avon to which he had been witness. He seemed a mighty ratling, har'em scar'em Gentleman, but talked so fluently that I had no trouble in contributing my mite towards keeping up the conversation, as he talked enough for 4, - & this I was prodigiously pleased at, as I was in an indolent mood, & not disposed to bear my share. I fancy, when he pleases, & thinks it worth while, he can be sensible & agreeable; - but all his desire then was to alarm Miss Weston, & persuade the Company she had been guilty of a thousand misdemeanours.

In the midst of this Rattle, Mrs Whalley proposed that Miss Thrale should go down stairs to hear a Miss Sage play upon the Harpsichord. Miss Sage is a Niece of Mrs Whalley, & about 9 years old. I offered to be of the Party, - Miss Weston joined us, as did the Miss Ansteys, & down we went. And terribly wearied was I! - She played a Lesson of Giordani's, that seemed to have no end, & repeated all the Parts into the Bargain! - And this, with various little English songs, detained us till we were summoned to the Carriage. I had an opportunity, however, of seeing something of (the) Miss Ansteys, - & 1 found them such precise, formal, composed & dull young Women, that the same opportunity also served to acquaint me that I never need desire to see any thing more of them.[46]

Neighbours in Royal Crescent (see Appendix 2)

Philip Thicknesse has already been mentioned. More respectable, though only slightly so, was Christopher Anstey at No.4, whose portrait, by William Hoarse, now hangs in the Bath Guildhall. Anstey had been born in 1724 in Cambridgeshire, the son of the Vicar of Brinkley, also named Christopher Anstey. The latter would have known Thomas Sedgwick's father; not only were they were subject to the same Bishop but John Whalley had been born only three miles from where Christopher Anstey senior was to become Rector. Christopher Anstey junior became a Fellow of King's College Cambridge in 1745 and would have known Professor Whalley as the Regius Professor of Divinity and Master of Peterhouse.

Royal Crescent, Bath.

In 1756, Anstey junior had married the daughter of a wealthy brewer and settled down to manage the estate his father-in-law had bequeathed him. Like Thomas Sedgwick, Christopher Anstey was a Cambridge scholar with an interest in poetry. After suffering a 'bilious fever' he visited Bath to take the waters and, on his return to Cambridge, had written the 'New Bath Guide'. This hugely popular work was a satirical review of Bath's fashionable society in verse.[47] It was first published in 1766 and was the author's only work of any consequence. The book eventually ran to 40 editions and was said to be an influence on the form adopted by WS Gilbert in his 'Bab Ballards'. It was because of its success that the Anstey the family moved to Bath in 1770.

In a letter from Bath dated August 3rd, 1779, Anstey writes to thank Thomas and his wife for providing his son with a 'continued (sic) round of pleasure and entertainment'.[48] This was almost certainly Arthur Anstey, who became an Attorney and Thomas Sedgwick Whalley's legal adviser.[49] The entertainment must have been at Langford Court since, after their marriage, it was the custom of the Whalleys to spend from June to October there. Christopher Anstey also

The Whalleys house in Royal Crescent – the second door from the left.

asks to be remembered to Thomas Sedgwick's mother, referring to her as *'my old and respected friend'*. This rather confirms that the two families were known to each other from their Cambridge days. In 1790, Thomas Sedgwick officiated in the marriage of Anstey's third daughter, Caroline, to another mutual friend, Henry Bosanquet, a barrister of Lincoln's Inn, who would later rent Langford Court from Whalley.[50] Having moved to Bath, Anstey gained the friendship of the actor/manager David Garrick, the playwright Richard Brinsley Sheridan, and Sir John and Lady Miller, whose poetry gatherings were a feature of the Bath season.

The history behind these poetical occasions is as follows: Sir John and Lady Miller had returned to Batheaston from Italy in 1759 with an Etruscan vase which had been dug up at Frascati. This was incorporated into a *Temple of Apollo* at their new home in Batheaston. Sometime after this, Mrs Miller started her poetical gatherings, which were certainly established by 1774. These were based initially on the *'Bouts Rimés'* poetry fashion brought by the then Mrs Miller from France. From December to May within the Bath season, Lady Miller would issue a general invitation to ladies and gentlemen of fashion to attend a fortnightly poetry festival at her house. Here the would-be poets found the Etruscan vase, set up on a modern altar in the bay window of the Batheaston villa. Each gentleman and lady was required to submit their poetical offering to it. The assembly having all contributed, Mr Miller selected a lady who would draw these out one at a time at random to be read aloud by a gentleman. After this, a small committee of six retired to an adjacent room to determine the four best submissions while food was served. The four chosen then identified themselves by their coded signatures and were crowned with myrtle by Mrs Miller. Initially this event was held on Fridays but, because of a clash with the Bath Ball, was later held on Thursday afternoons. Winners were expected to display their wreaths or sprigs of myrtle at the Ball the following day.[51]

It is very likely that it was through Anstey that Thomas Sedgwick Whalley was soon contributing to these poetical gatherings. In 1775, the first of four volumes of selected poems from these occasions was published and proved very popular. Both Whalley and Anstey contributed to these. Hill Wickham includes a letter from Lady Miller to Thomas dated November 3rd, 1780, urging him to be available to attend the first day of the winter season on 21st December.[52] These occasions brought him into contact with Anna Seward, who regarded herself as patroness of the poetic muse, and was to prove to be a lifelong friend and admirer. Her father was a minor Canon of Litchfield Cathedral.

Lady Miller's Etruscan vase.

33

The Theatre and Mrs Siddons

It is clear that Thomas Sedgwick was already writing plays in the early years of his marriage and would have attended the theatre at Bath during the season.

The plays of Thomas Sedgwick Whalley
- The Fatal Kiss, first published anonymously 1779, then under his own name in 1781
- Edwy and Edilda, 1779
- The Castel of Montval, 1781
- Kenneth and Fenella, 1809

Hill Wickham states that Thomas Sedgwick's house in Bath brought him into contact with Mrs Siddons,[53] who at this time was still a struggling actress, touring the country with her actor husband. The couple had arrived in Bath in 1778 and were members of the Bristol / Bath Company from 1778 until 1782. Her first recorded performance as leading lady in Bath was on Saturday, October 24th, 1778, in '*The provoked husband*' by Vanbrugh, a popular play there.[54]

Thomas may well have met Mrs Siddons the following May (1779) when Hannah More's play '*The Fatal Falsehood*' was performed for the first time. During the next three years, Mrs Siddons made a sufficient name for herself among London visitors to Bath to be invited by Garrick to join the Drury Lane Company. By the time of her Bath benefit performance, on June 17th, 1782, she and the Whalleys were firm, if not close, friends.[55] His play '*The Castle of Montval*' had been written in 1781 and he clearly hoped it might be performed at Bath.[56] He wrote a poem '*Verses Addressed to Mrs Siddons on being engaged at Drury Lane*' when her move to London was announced late in 1781. An advertisement, doubtless inserted by himself, mentions that '*The Reverend Mr Whalley was also the author of Edwy and Edilda, etc. etc.*' By that time Thomas Sedgwick had unsuccessfully sought the support of Mrs Siddons and others to get the play performed by the company at Bath but '*The Castle of Montval*' was finally put on at Drury Lane in July 1799. According to his brother, the Reverend Richard Chaple Whalley, Thomas Sedgwick, who was then living at Hampton Court, was in high anxiety about this production for many weeks. Richard always disapproved of someone in Thomas' position in life ever having written such a play. He was now Rector of Horsington, having abandoned an idea of becoming an artist and taken advantage of the offer of a living from his brother-in-law, James Wickham.[57]

In a letter to his niece, Frances Sullivan, née Sage, written July 22nd, 1799, he says:

> *Your uncle Sedgwick, I suppose you know, has been in the neighbourhood of London for some time, staking his reputation on the reception of a play. T'was a sad losing game, for, whatever the fate of the play, his reception with all good and wise people was sure to suffer; but our vanities and our views blind us to a degree that is hardly credible or conceivable.*[58]

There seems to have been some doubt as to whether the play would ever appear. Mr Siddons wrote to Thomas Sedgwick on December 15th, 1797, describing a rival version of the play, by Matthew (Monk) Lewis, which appeared under the title of '*The Castle Spectre*'. However, he also speaks of a promise which the Drury Lane theatre had clearly given to Thomas Sedgwick to stage the play which Mr Siddons expected they would keep.[59] In the event, when the play did finally appear, 18 months later, despite efforts by Anna Seward to ensure all the appropriate influential members of Society were present,[60] and despite having Mrs Siddons in the leading role as had been planned, the critics were not favourably impressed. The play was only given nine performances and was never put on again. This must have been particularly galling for Thomas Sedgwick, since the young author of its rival '*The Castle Spectre*' had only graduated from Oxford three years before. In a period when very few plays reached ten performances in a season, the rival version by Monk had been staged 47 times and even now remains on the reading list of many universities as the archetypical gothic play! Anna Seward's predictable glowing letter of congratulation to Thomas, in which she discounted the newspaper criticisms, can have been of little comfort to him.[61]

By this time, Thomas' career in the church had advanced significantly. In 1777, on the death of Samuel Hood, he was appointed Prebend of Combe XIII at Wells, an appointment he held until shortly before his death. This would now require regular visits to Wells and it is of significance that his near neighbour in Royal Crescent was Dr Edward Cooper, also a Prebend of Wells (Holcombe 1770-1792), and also Jane Austin's uncle. Whether the two families knew each other is discussed in Appendix 4.

The seat of Prebend Combe XIII in the Wells Chapter House.

FAMILY TRAGEDY

T HE DEEP FONDNESS between Thomas and his sister has already been mentioned and this, and their stream of affectionate correspondence, continued after their marriages. The Sage's very full social life led to their two children, Frances and her younger sister Emily, spending much time at Bath with Thomas and his wife.

In the summer of 1773, Isaac Sage was clearly not intending to return to India. His wife speaks to Thomas of her husband's impatience to complete the purchase of the Thornhill Estate, whose home farm they proposed keeping in hand *'for profit and amusement'.*[62]

Quite who persuaded Isaac to return to India, or when he agreed to do so, is not known. Perhaps the possibility of his return was raised during the Christmas of 1773, which Isaac and his wife spent at Lovell Hill, home of Hugh

Thornhill originally built by Sir James Thornhill the famous painter.

Watts (see Chapter 1). On the other hand, in a letter to Thomas a few weeks earlier, Elizabeth had said that Isaac had a great deal of business to attend to in London, so perhaps it was raised before then.[63]

There had been a severe famine in Bengal between 1769 and 1773, where the population had declined by a third. It was argued that the activities of the East India Company officials, using their monopoly rights on trade and land tax for personal benefit, were partly to blame. So perhaps the company sought a proven honest and steady servant to take matters in hand.

Isaac seems to have left for India some time in 1774. In a letter to her brother Thomas dated October 1st, 1775, Elizabeth reports that she has just received news from her husband which he had written the previous February *'on the boat going up to Patna'*. Since it usually took six months to get to India, this would suggest his departure was the mid-summer of 1774.

By March 1775, Isaac was ensconced as Governor of West Bengal and Chief Factor in Patna dealing with the complexities of managing the opium trade, which at that time contributed 25% of the East India Company profits and which would lead ultimately to the Opium Wars. Various letters to and from him are known.[64,65] In the same month back in England, his three-year-old daughter Emily, Thomas Sedgwick's goddaughter, had died. There is no mention of this event in any of the correspondence which his great nephew Hill Wickham later published. Given the grief which Elizabeth and Thomas would have shared, this is so out of character as to be impossible. Most likely Hill Wickham, with his Victorian sensibilities, omitted such letters as being too personal for inclusion. In the next recorded letter dated October 1st, 1775, Elizabeth has already decided to join her husband in India. Although she writes from Thornhill, she reports that she has already been on board the boat which will take her to India:

Mr Wheeler who is one of the Directors (of the East India Company) and was Chairman when Mr Sage was appointed and was most helpful in making arrangements... [66]

The helpful director was Edward Wheeler, a director of the East India Company from 1765-1776 and its Chairman from 1773-74.

In a subsequent letter to her brother-in-law, the lawyer James Wickham, she says she wishes to let Thornhill House and gives very clear details of payments which were to be made to her brother Thomas for her daughter Fanny's upkeep out of the anticipated rent. These were £100 per annum, plus £10 for the cost of six-year-old Fanny's nurse and £25 for Mrs Mazell, who one assumes was her governess. In addition, he was to reimburse his brother-in-law '*Tom*' for '*any little bills*' which he might send him. [67]

This advertisement appeared in the Salisbury & Winchester Journal in October, 1775:[68]

STALBRIDGE, DORSET

To be LETT, and entered upon immediately, ready furnished, THORNHILL HOUSE, belonging to Isaac Sage, Esq.; consisting of a hall, breakfast parlour, dining parlour, house-keeper's room, servant's hall, butler's pantry, kitchen, and other convenient offices on the first floor; a gallery (ninety-three feet by twenty-one),[69] drawing room, dressing room, and six handsome bed chambers adjoining, on the second floor; stabling for 14 horses, double coach house, kitchen garden, with walls planted with young fruit trees.

The house has been lately elegantly fitted up, and furnished, is pleasantly situated, and commands rich extensive views, and is within the parish of Stalbridge in the county of Dorset, distant from Sherborne 6 miles, Blandford 12, and Shaftesbury 14.

The land belonging to, and lying round the house, consisting of about 500 acres of arable, meadow and pasture, to be also let, and entered upon immediately, or at Lady-day next, or the whole or any part of it may be taken with the house, and the Stock thereon bought at a fair appraisement.

Further particulars may be had of Francis Edwards Whalley, Esq.; of Winscombe, near Axbridge, or of Mr Wickham, of Frome, Somerset. - Mr Clift, at the house.

It is hardly surprising that Elizabeth should want to join her husband but as Hill Wickham states it was also unwise for someone who had always had a delicate constitution to travel to India.[70] Perhaps she was aware of this. Her letter to Thomas Sedgwick from Pall Mall, dated December 6th, 1775, in which she apologises for having no time to visit him before leaving, was to prove sadly prophetic:

> *My spirits keep up; nor should I cast one look behind but for the friends I leave, they ever must be dear! No time or distance can remove their idea, or the remembrance of the tenderness I have received, particularly from my dear Sedgwick and my sister* (i.e. Thomas' wife). *All the love you would continue to show me, bestow on my poor Fanny, your Fanny now; I give her up to you with this confidence, that she will never feel the loss of father or mother while under your care. Protect her innocence and foster her virtues.* [71]

Elizabeth sailed from Gravesend at the end of December, 1775, and left Portsmouth on January 6th, 1776. Her vivid descriptions of her six month voyage, via Madeira and Cape Town, deserve special mention. They demonstrate her intelligence, education and vivacity as well as the closeness of her family. It is interesting to note that all these are addressed to her sister, Mary Wickham, the editor's great grandmother. She must have written similar letters to Thomas Sedgwick but these are not included. In the one letter written by her to Thomas from London at this time, one month before she sailed and dated November 2nd, 1775, she asks him to send her 12 dozen bottles of Bristol (Hotwells) water in two chests. She points out that while she could purchase these in London she '*could not depend in its being fresh; and it would answer little purpose to carry it stale*'.[72] Such concerns were well known and, in 1789, the Merchant Venturers had received a letter of complaint about Bristol water bought in London asking that, in future, the retailer be denied further supplies.

To her surprise, Elizabeth Sage found the sea passage suited her very well. She reported that she did not suffer from seasickness, was putting on weight and was feeling better than she had been since the birth of her '*dear Fanny*'.[73] This implies that she had been unwell for the six years since Frances' birth. She reached India in the autumn of 1776 and, in a long letter to her sister Susan, (Mrs Wickham), dated 1st November, she describes her life there:

You may perhaps be surprised when I tell you that to me a life of parade and state which Mr Sage's consequence here give me is irksome. Yet so it is; nor do I derive any satisfaction but from his society and tenderness, which is, if possible, more than ever; nor do we feel a pleasure independent of eachother.

An Indian life is chiefly divided betwixt dressing and sleeping. My style of passing the time is as follows:- We rise pretty early, when Mr Sage mounts his horse, and I pursue exercise of walking, during which I could wish you to see my attendants. One man walks by my side with an umbrella, also another kind of state servant (which are perfect shadows of their mistress), and behind him four others with long canes. Thus in procession I take my ramble till breakfast, after which Mr Sage pays me a visit, for we do not take this meal together, nor are we in the same house. I have apartments of my own, which consist of a bed chamber and three small rooms adjoining (one of them a bathing room), also a very good room which Mr Sage built for me, when he first heard of my coming out (this must have been by a letter sent shortly before she sailed) *He has always company for breakfast and the rest of his morning is engaged in business. I spend mine reading, writing and the grand study of dress to prepare for which I have always three tailors (who are men that work very neatly) employed. Mondays and Thursday are council days when Mr Sage has a public table: on those days I eat in my own room; on other days I dine with him. After dinner we go to bed, rise again about five, dress for the evening and take an airing in the carriage till tea. But as the day closes in this part of the world very early, our rides are somewhat singular. As it is generally pretty dark before we get home, on our return we are met by ten or dozen servants with flambeaux, and, instead of horsemen attending the carriage a man runs by the side of each horse, which they are so accustomed to, that they keep pace with them and will go for ten miles without being out of breath or fatigued. On our public days I join the evening party, which is large enough to make five or six tables, and we play cards till supper.*

She later adds:

You may imagine us fixed here for some years but that is far from our intention. Had I not taken this resolution of coming out, Mr Sage would have set sail for

Europe probably in the very ship which conveys this (letter) *to you, unable as he told me to support a longer separation. He was settling his affairs to return when the account of my intention arrived and he left it entirely to me to resolve whether I would go this season or the next; the latter I preferred both from a pecuniary motive, and as my mind rejected, however pleasant the voyage had been, a repetition of it so soon. One year my dear sister will soon elapse...* [74]

However, this was not to be as she soon fell ill. There was a low life expectancy among East India Company employees and during the period 1707-1775, when it appointed 640 writers, 58% of them died.[75] Hill Wickham states that, because of Elizabeth's ill heath, Isaac was forced to relinquish his lucrative post and return home to England.[76] Other accounts say she returned to England in 1777, followed shortly by her husband. However records show that she died in Bath on December 17th, 1778.[13] This is likely to have been in her brother Thomas' house in Royal Crescent since the Sages had no permanent house there. This would have been the logical place to go to. Not only was her surviving daughter, Frances, living there with the Whalleys but, during the winter season in Bath, there would have been the best doctors of the time, serving the needs of the wealthy infirm. Sadly, Hill Wickham includes no correspondence of any kind for the period from November 1776 until August 1779, nine months after her death.

Elizabeth was buried in the Lady Chapel of Wells Cathedral on 24th December, 1778. One suspects the hand of Thomas Sedgwick, as a prebend of Wells Cathedral, in seeing that his sister was buried there, rather than at St Cuthbert's Church, Wells, where she had been married nine years earlier. It is also very likely that Thomas arranged for the placing of the memorial tablet which his great nephew Hill Wickham would restore in 1867.[77]

On the death of his sister, Hill Wickham states that Thomas transferred his affections to her daughter, his niece Frances Sage,[78] who thereafter spent a great deal of her time with him and his wife in Bath. This is certainly borne out by subsequent events. A year later, sometime in 1779, Thomas paid £50 for a portrait to be painted of the nine-year-old Frances by George Romney. Such a portrait does still exist and was sold by Sotheby's to a buyer in South America in July 1987. Sadly, a letter forwarded by them to the new owner failed to elicit any response.

The memorial tablet to Elizabeth Sage and her second daughter Emily in Wells Cathedral cloister.
It is surmounted by the Whalley and Sage coat of arms.

Tablet in East Cloister

Burial register of Cathedral
states Dec 24 1778 buried in
Lady Chapel

Near this place lies the body of
Elizabeth Sage
who departed this life the 17th December 1778
aged 33 years.
In testimony of most sincere affection
for an amiable, tender, virtuous wife
her disconsolate husband Isaac Sage Esqre
of Thornhill in the county of Dorset
caused this memorial to be erected.
With her mother lies also the Body of
Emily Sage
daughter of Isaac and Elizabeth Sage
who departed this life the 27th March 1775
in the 3rd year of her age.
Restored by the Revd Hill D. Wickham.
Rector of Horsington
Great nephew of the above Elizabeth Sage 1867.

A transcript of the memorial above.

FRANCES GROWING UP

QUITE HOW MUCH time the young Frances spent with the Whalleys after the death of her mother is not clear. Little more is heard of Isaac Sage after the death of his wife apart from his visit to join the Whalleys on the continent (see below). Wickham states that Isaac never remarried. No evidence to the contrary has been found, yet two under-age daughters, Marianne and Julia, are recorded in Isacc's Will, dated October 4th, 1811, which was written at Gatton Park, a 250-acre estate in Surrey, now occupied by the Royal Alexandra and Albert School. This date is of significance since his son Frederick had died in August and is buried in Gatton church.[79, 80]

Certainly, Frances spent some time with her father in London and also at their estate at Thornhill, Dorset, as she was growing up. Her father would become the High Sheriff of Dorset in 1784,[81] but there are no details of Frances' early education. Had Thomas Sedgwick any influence on this? He certainly was a highly educated man whose views on women's education are likely to have been those of the bluestocking circle with which he was now associated. It is also clear that Frances' mother had been well educated and it would have been her wish that Frances was no less enlightened, but whatever influences were bought to bear as she grew up, there is no evidence that Frances acquired a circle of intellectual friends in later life.

In early 1783, the preliminary Articles of Peace were signed at Versailles and the Whalleys began to think of moving to the continent for an extended holiday.[82] By this time, Thomas' lifestyle was beginning to eat into his wife's fortune and, in that year, the Whalleys had mortgaged Langford Court, together with two houses and approximately 270 acres of land, for £3,000.[83] Langford Court was now let to General Gunning,[84] and their house in Royal Crescent was also let.[85] Although Hill Wickham states that their tour of Europe was undertaken *'at no mean expense'*, living on the continent was cheaper and would have permitted financial recovery from what had been a period of lavish entertainment at their house in Bath.[86] Thomas might also have wished to show his wife France, as well as introduce her to the influential friends he had made on his Grand Tour 15 years before.

Travels on the continent

It is possible to follow the Whalleys' movements though France, Savoy, Northern Italy, and Switzerland from the accounts given in the three journals which Thomas Sedgwick kept,[87] and from the letters which he and his wife sent home to friends and relatives. The first tour was made from Chambery, which was then the capital of Savoy, but there is no record of how the Whalleys had made their way there but it seems, from Hill Wickham's introduction to his two volume account of his great uncle's life, that they had done so via Paris and Versailles, where Marie Antoinette had afterwards referred to Thomas Whalley as *'le bel Anglais'*.[88,89]

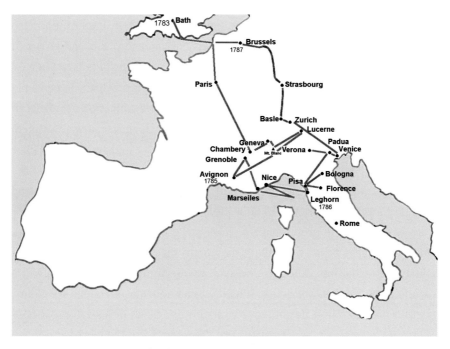

The Whalleys' travels in Europe 1784 – 1787.

Thomas' first recorded letter from the continent to his niece is from Chambery, and dated July 27th, 1784.[90] Frances was then aged just 15, but it is clear that there had been earlier correspondence. It would seem, from the references made in the letter that, at this time, Frances was living mainly with her father, but was also leading an active social life in Bath. There is no evidence that her father had a permanent house in Bath but, since Lowndes states that Frances continued to live in the Whalley's house, [91] perhaps it was let to her father. In 1784, the 15-year-old spent the winter *'under the protection of Mrs Blair'*, something of which her aunt Mrs Whalley thoroughly approved.[92] This was possibly Mrs Patricia Blair, the widow of the Rev Dr John Blair, Prebend of Westminster but whose family seat was Balthayock in Scotland, to whom Mrs Whalley asks Frances to pass on her compliments.[93]

In February, 1785, we find the only recorded rebuke from Mrs Whalley, who gently chides Frances from Avignon for not replying to earlier letters:

I know the goodness of your heart too well my beloved Frances, to ever suspect that your silence proceeds from want of affection towards an uncle and aunt who love you with all the tenderness of parents........

But I cannot say I so entirely acquit you of negligence... for depriving me for six long months....of the pleasure of hearing from you.[94]

However, by May, 1785, all is restored following receipt of Fanny's *'most affectionate letter'*.[95] Mrs Whalley, now writing from near Lisle, says:

I cannot quit the subject of your present establishment, without repeating my dearest girl, the joy it gives me that the Almighty has blessed you with a parent whose every wish seems to centre in your happiness nor does he think any expense too great that may contribute to your advantage.

She then goes on to tempt providence by adding :

I am sure your heart must expand with filial love and gratitude towards him, and make no doubt but you will in return be everything, both in conduct and accomplishment, that he can wish - that you will gild his days with joy in the meridian of life and crown his latter years with peace.

She concludes her letter with:

I will therefore bid you adieu my beloved child. Do not let the term give you umbrage, for I know we are very delicate on certain points at 15 (years of age); but I will always consider myself as your mother, if I live to see you thirty since I never can yield myself second in affection towards you to any human being but your father as believe me every maternal feeling every tender solicitude for your welfare expands the breast of your ever affectionate.

Eliza Whalley

In the same letter, she had expressed satisfaction that Frances was now so happily placed with Mrs Gordon, to whom she claims to be distantly related. The Honorable Mrs Gordon was the granddaughter of Lord Portsmouth and the daughter of Lord Lymington; we are told that Mrs Whalley's late father had been on intimate terms with the latter and his brother Colonel Wallop.[96] Mrs Gordon at that time received a few young ladies into her house *'who wished to profit by London masters'*.[97] Whether this was in music or painting is unclear but in a later letter Thomas Sedgwick includes many references to the paintings he and his wife are seeing and adds that he is glad that Fanny's drawing and instrumental music are not being neglected. Certainly by this time Frances was a becoming an excellent harpsicord player. Five years later, one of Anna Seward's friends declared that she and her husband could not distinguish Frances' playing from that of the professional player Mrs Miles.[98] (Mrs Miles, née Guest, taught piano and appeared in Rauzzini's concerts in Bath in 1790 and was later appointed teacher to Princesses Amalie and Charlotte).[99]

It has been said that no child is strong enough to bear the love of two parents alone. Frances had lost her younger sister and mother but, as has been seen, had acquired two indulgent would-be parents in addition to her own wealthy father. In these earlier exchanges there are pointers to a degree of indulgence on the part of her father and Mrs Whalley which would not bode well for the future. To this, add that of her uncle in a letter dated October,

1784, from Avignon:

Though I consider you as your aunt's correspondent, yet my dearest Fanny, I cannot deny myself the pleasure of now and then encroaching upon her rights, and assuring you, with my own pen, that absence only serves to increase my affection for you. It is impossible, my darling niece, to describe the satisfaction that the account of your merits gives me from all quarters. To see you grow up amiable and accomplished has always been my chief ambition, and I cannot hear that you are equal to my fondest hopes without the most sensible joy and pride. How delightful also must it be to you, my sweet girl, to see yourself as the blessing of your dear father's life; and that you find it in your power, by your talents and your tenderness, to recompense him for all his cares, and almost restore to him all the domestic delights and comforts that he lost in losing your charming and excellent mother. What happiness to myself, as well as him, to see her living again in you; to see all her graces and all her virtues blooming and ripening with your years![100]

and later:

It is impossible to tell you how much delighted your excellent aunt was with your letter. Not only the tender regard glowing so artlessly throughout its pages, but the style also in which it was expressed, charmed her. Indeed my dear it was convincing proof to us that Mrs Gordon's letters are full of graces, and that you have profited by them. It is truly kind in (sic) her to have corresponded with you, and shows not only her attention to your improvement, but that she knows also how to appreciate your understanding, and draw out those emulations which are the spur to excellence and which excite us and enable us to go on from strength to strength. While you are emulating the charms of Mrs Gordon's style, think also my sweet girl that you are imitating that of your dear and incomparable mother, who eminently excelled in letter writing, and whose example in every respect it should be your pride, as it will be your advantage to follow.[101]

Not perhaps the sort of thing one should be telling a 15-year-old!

Return to England

Finally, in early summer of 1786, the Whalleys set out on their return journey which would take them back to England the following year. From Italy they travelled through the Tyrol to Switzerland, arriving in Zurich in June and then progressed down the Rhine, via Basle, arriving in Strasbourg a month later.[102] From here the Whalleys wrote to Frances Sage at Thornhill in June, 1786, and in July to her uncle Joseph's house in London. By this time, it had been agreed that Frances and her father would join the Whalleys in Brussels on 13th or 14th August. Thomas adds a footnote to Mrs Whalley's letter of July 23rd, telling Frances not to forget her Italian songs and her *'drawing apparatus'*.[103] By early August the Whalleys are in Malines (now known as Mechelen, lying between Brussels and Antwerp). It would seem that it had been the Whalley's original intention to include Holland in their final travels but this idea was abandoned, probably because of their niece's arrival. Hill Wickham says that Frances spent 1787-8 with the Whalleys in Brussels and, while there, they made the acquaintance of the Duke d'Arenberg and his daughter, who invited the Whalleys and their niece to visit his country seat. This would mark the beginning of Frances' lifelong friendship with Princess D'Arenberg who was of the same age.[104] (See Appendix 3)

Hill Wickham says that, while at Brussels, the Whalleys 'met up again' with Mrs Piozzi. This was the former Mrs Thrale who had recently remarried following the death of her first husband and was now on an extended European tour with her Italian husband, who had been her daughter's music teacher. However, Mrs Piozzi's letter to Mr Lysons, dated 11th May, 1786, reveals that her first meeting with the Whalleys had been in Venice.[105] When they met up in Brussels at the beginning of 1787, Mrs Piozzi records:

> *Mr Merry lodges in our Hotel here and we talk of you (i.e. Mr William Parson to whom the letter of February 5th is addressed) and Mrs and Mrs Greathead by the hour. The Whalleys too help to make our Time pass very agreeably; I always loved 'em, and they are grown more amiable now than ever.* [106]

In their footnote, Bloom and Bloom refer to a letter from her daughter "Queeny" (Hester Maria Thrale), who, three days later, wrote:

Here are crowds of English here - we wait for a fine assembly at Mrs Whalley's.[107]

From this it would seem that, as in Bath, such assemblies were the way in which the Whalleys made connections with the many influential people they met on their travels. Indeed, given the timing of this particular assembly, it may be that this was the one where they met the D'Arenbergs.

The Whalleys continental tour ended in early summer, 1787. Thomas Sedgwick's first letter to Frances from England is dated June 15th, 1787, and is addressed to her father's house in St. James Street, London. In this letter, Thomas Sedgwick alludes to her possible marriage. She would then have been 18-years-old:

> *Young Horner is now at Wells, and who knows but that Frank may bring him to you in his hand. I say this to prepare you in case of accidents, and that you may have time to consult your heart at leisure. God direct you for your happiness, my dear girl. If that is secured I care not how, or by whom.*[108]

This was likely to have been Francis Horner (1763-1813), related to the ancient Somerset family of Mells Park to whom Sir John Cox Hippisley was also a member, and a friend of the Sage family. This marriage clearly did not happen.

The miniature overleaf of Frances Sage by Cosway, as engraved by Joseph Brown, is from Hill Wickham's book. He suggests that the miniature was painted in 1787 when she would have been 18-years-old. He also says that there was a full-length portrait of her by Romney made at this time.[109] Neither has been located.

Frances Sage, perhaps 18-years-old.

It is difficult to judge Frances' character nearing adult life. There are no letters from her included in Hill Wickham's biography of her uncle and one has to therefore gain an idea of her character from the eight letters to her written by Thomas Sedgwick and his wife. Thomas claims, in his letter to his niece of October 6th, that she is growing up amiable and accomplished and acquiring all the graces and virtues of her mother.[110] Clearly, she was accomplished but one gets the impression that she was now a spirited, independent and worldly young lady having something of the character of Jane Austen's Mary Crawford.[111]

CHAPTER 5

MENDIP LODGE AND ITS DEVELOPMENT

W HEN, IN THE early summer of 1787, Thomas and Elizabeth returned to England, Langford Court was still let,[112] and although Colonel Gunning would leave the house in June the following year,[113] it seems the Whalleys now had no intention of returning to live there.[114] Thus, in 1790, Langford Court was re-let for a further three years to Whalley's friend, the lawyer Henry Bosanquet (1760-1816).[115] This was shortly after Thomas had conducted the marriage ceremony of Henry to Christopher Anstey's 3rd daughter, Caroline. Eventually, in 1804, John Hiley Addington, brother of the Prime Minister Lord Sidmouth, would buy the Langford Court and its estate.

Thomas' account of his travels on the continent shows that he was deeply affected by the scenery of Savoy:

> *Amongst my stroll, and a little after my arrival in that lovely and sublime country, I described a whitened cottage, smiling sweetly through its walnut shade on the side of a verdant hill with a view equally picturesque and noble...[116]*

This seems to have inspired him to create his own English version of such a scene on the north slope of the Mendips and, sometime in 1788, Thomas set about building his "cottage", a new summer residence above Langford Court. It is not clear if this was a completely new construction or, more likely, modification of an existing building, as the sale map of 1844 shows a "Weeks's Cottage" above the house, of which no trace now remains.

In May, 1789, Thomas was writing to Fanny apologising for his delay in writing to her:

You may imagine my dearest Fanny, that a cottager has abundance of time at his command. No such thing I assure you. It has been in my head long since to answer your sweet letter; but the saw on one side and a mason's trowel on the other, gardening here and building there, have still prevented me from paying a debt due to affection and urged by inclination.

This time her address, presumably that of her father, was George Street, Hanover Square. He goes on:

When all these hurries and flurries are over.........you shall come and be as much the shepherdess as you please; and feed the lambs and sing with the birds and lead about a lap dog in a rose-coloured ribbon and be all over sentiment and romance.

More significant to her future, bearing in mind she would be married almost exactly a year later, Thomas adds:

But a shepherd you must bring with you, if any such can be found in your sphere, for here we have none that will answer your ideas. Country shepherds, alas are in these our iron days mere clowns, with clod pates and filthy faces unknowing of garlands and crooks and pretty fancies. I am glad you and Mr -------- are so rational in your tête a têtes. Reason is so often banished on such occasions.[117]

Edmund Rack, writing in 1787 (which must have been before the house was completed, since he died in that year), describes the house as a neat white cottage, with an entrance leading into a properly furnished kitchen from which a narrow staircase ascended to an upper room.[118] In September the following year when the Whalleys visited their friend Anna Seward at Lichfield, it would seem the work on the house and surrounding garden was still not quite complete, since she says in a letter to Mr Newton:

The former (i.e. Thomas Sedgwick), engaged in building and opening, a little Edenic habitation in a bloomy wilderness, could only stay a week.[119]

It appears that the original cottage had a thatched roof. Benjamin Edward Somers reports that his grandfather Benjamin (1782-1848), who would eventually buy the house, was present as a young boy playing on the Bowling Green (which starts just out of sight to the right in the picture below) when the cottage "burnt down".[120] Sarah, the widow of Edward Somers, had moved to Springhead Farm, just below the house, with her three children sometime after the death of her husband in 1790,[121] the family having been adopted by Thomas Sedgwick and his wife. The date of the fire is confirmed in a letter from Mrs Pennington to Mrs Piozzi, dated 7th June, 1793, when she reported that it was caused by the carelessness of a servant. Fortunately, the fire occurred during the day and so assistance was soon obtained. One assumes this would have come from the Somers family and staff at Springhead Farm. No lives were put in danger but there was £200 worth of damage and Mrs Whalley returned to Bath while the repairs were being undertaken.[122]

The house seems to have been added to intermittently until at least 1791 and so ended up more than twice the size of the original building. This is clear from later photographs of the rear of the house.

The rear of the completed Mendip Lodge. The original "cottage" is likely to have been the Gothic building on the left.

The earliest known picture of Mendip Lodge, published by J. Rutter, 1829.

Descriptions of the completed Mendip Lodge

When the cottage was finally completed, Thomas and his wife resumed their former custom of spending the summer there and the winter season in Bath. He clearly now regarded the former as his home (*'Bath is but my visit, the dear Lodge is my home'*).[123]

As no plans exist for Mendip Lodge at any stage in its evolution, one has to be content with later photographs and contemporary descriptions, the earliest of which occurs in a letter which Anna Seward wrote to Lady Gresley from Mendip Lodge, then Langford Cottage, dated July 30th, 1791. In this is included a report of her journey from Tewkesbury via Gloucester to Langford although, the exact date of this visit is not given. Perhaps she came as far as Churchill Cross on the Bristol to Bridgwater turnpike by stagecoach:

At ten o'clock Mr Whalley arrived in his chaise, to conduct me to his Eden, among the Mendip mountains, Singularly, and beyond my high-raised expectations, beautiful I did indeed find it; situated, built, furnished, and adorned in the very spirit of poetic enthusiasm, and polished simplicity. It is about twelve years since Mr Whalley began to cover with a profusion of trees and shrubs, one of these vast hills, then barren like its brethren. The plantations seem already to have attained their full size, strength, and exuberance of foliage.

By the addition of another horse, to help the chaise-horses, we ascended the sylvan steep [this would have been up what is now the bridleway known as Stoney Path]. *At about two-thirds of its height on a narrow terrace, stands the dear white cottage, whose polished graces seem smilingly to deride its name, though breathing nothing heterogeneous to cottage simplicity. The first floor consists of a small hall, with a butler's pantry to the right, and good kitchen to the left; housekeeper's room beyond that; scullery behind the kitchen; the offices at a little distance detached from the house, many steps below this bank. and screened from sight by trees. The second floor contains, in front, to the north west, three lightsome, lovely, though not large, apartments, whose spacious sashes are of the Gothic form. These are the dining-room, the drawing-room and elegant boudoir beyond, all opening through each other. My apartment from which I write, is behind the boudoir; its window, at the end of the house, looking to the east and upon a steep lawn, sprinkled over with larches, poplars, and woodbines, excluded by a circular plantation from all prospect of the magnificent vale upon which the front rooms look down, in instant and almost perpendicular descent. A gravel walk winds up this secluded lawn to the mountain top. Mr and Mrs Whalley, and their other guests sleep in the attics. The wide-extended vale beneath us has every possible scenic beauty, excepting only the meanders of a river. Scarce two hundred yards from the villa, on the left hand, a bare brown mountain intersects this, its woody neighbour, and towers equal heights. The protection it extends from the north-west wind has been everything to Mr Whalley, as to the growth and health of his plantations. Sloping its giant's foot to the valley, it finely contrasts, with barren sterility, the rich cultivation of the valley below, and the lavish umbrage which curtains these slopes.*

With the sort of sensation that a beauteous country girl, in the first glow of youth and health, surveys an antiquated dowager of rank and riches, seems this little villa to look down on the large stone mansion of Langford Court, the property of Mr and Mrs Whalley, and their former residence. It stands in the valley, about half a mile from us encircled by its fine lawn of two hundred acres, planted and adorned with great taste. Yet more immediately below us, nestles in a wood, the village of Langford. The smoke of its farms and cottages curling amongst the trees at early morn, imparts the glow of vitality and cheerfulness to our romantic retirement. I climb, by seven o'clock in a morning, the highest terrace, and 'drink the spirit of the mountain gale' which seems to invigorate my whole frame, and give my lungs the freest respiration. Never before did I breathe, for any continuance, an atmosphere so sublimated. The extensive vale finely breaks into inequalities by knolls and dingles. The beautiful fields, wearing from the late rains, the brightest verdure, have wave outlines of plenteous hedge-moss and appear, by their depth from the eye, shining and smooth as the lawns of our nobility. They are interspersed with thick and dark, though not large, woods. The whole wide expanse is dotted over by white rough-cast cottages, and here and there a village-spire and squiral chateau.

Fifteen miles in width and about seven distant from this elevation, the Bristol channel lies, a sheet of silver stretched longitudinally over the vale. Beyond, we plainly discern the Welsh coast, whose mountains bound the horizon.

Mr Whalley's walks and bowers are finely diversified.

"Shade above shade, a woody theatre".

The several terraces ascending over each other are connected by steep winding paths for the active, and by grassy steps for the feeble. These terraces are so variously planted and disposed, as to avoid all that sameness to which, from their situation, they were liable; now secluded and gloomy, now admitting the rich world below to burst upon the eye. Hermitages and caves cut in the rocky steeps contain rustic seats dedicated to favourite friends, by poetic inscriptions; one to Mrs Siddons; another to Miss Hannah More; another to the accomplished Mrs Jackson of Bath; one to Mr Whalley's venerable mother; another to Mr Inman, the excellent clergyman of this parish; one to Sophia Weston (later to become Mrs Pennington), and one to myself. These grottos relieve us perpetually by their seats amidst ascents so nearly perpendicular.

Mendip Lodge, as it was in about 1923, viewed from just inside the park.

Mendip Lodge from the Northwest, as it was in about 1923.

'Mont Blanc'- A late photograph of Mendip Lodge seen from the west; part of the new drive can be seen on the left.

Mr Whalley's mother is here, a miracle at eighty five, of clear intellects, upright activity, and graceful manners; also Miss Davey, a fine young woman, related to Mrs Whalley; but charming Sophia [Weston] is not here; the scanty number of these pretty bed-chambers forbids the accommodation of more than two or three friends at the utmost. [124]

In 1801, Hannah More, now one of his closest friends and neighbours, suggested that Thomas should adopt the name of *'Mendip Lodge'* as being more appropriate for what was now an impressive country house.[125] She called the house *'Mont Blanc'* as its frontage was rendered and painted white – presumably with lime wash – and could be seen by her across the valley. A later letter from Anna Seward to Mrs Powys, dated October, 1804, reflects on the improvements made to the house since her earlier visit in 1791.[126]

While Thomas Sedgwick and his wife usually spent the winter in Bath, there is one description of Mendip Lodge in winter which he sent to Anna Seward who, in turn, forwarded it to her friend Miss Stokes in December, 1791.

Our beloved cottage still has charms for us. Use cannot pall nor custom stale its infinite variety. Elevated as we are, the south-west hurricanes pass innoxious over our heads, because we have plantations of evergreens, as you know, and terraces that rise above us to nearly the mountain's summit; and because the more lofty mountain which intersects ours on the left (i.e. to the west of Stoney Lane), *forms our sheltering screen. But those hurricanes rush with tenfold violence through the vale beneath us, while our comforts within are undamped by the rain, and unchilled by the frost. A thousand cottages, undescried in leafy summer, now shew their white cheerful faces. The brook, which you called a nothing, and which, during the softer season, is, in truth, most shallow and simple, runs now expanded, and foams with turbulent pride at our feet; while the more distance moors, covered with water, perfectly resemble a majestic river, rolling between us and the sea.*[127]

Quite why the Whalleys should have been there at this time, and not at their house in Bath, is not clear.

Anna Seward's fuller account of the house,[128] when at its zenith, can be supplemented by a number of other descriptions. Sarah Siddons described the house as her '*Castle in the Air*', and the Bishop of London, Dr Porteous, said he had never witnessed an entertainment so perfect in its appointment. Thomas De Quincey gives a less complimentary account of the house. This seems to have been written from memory, since it was published almost 10 years after Thomas Sedgwick's death:

From the Hotwells, Mrs Siddons had been persuaded to honour with her company certain Dr Wh--- whose splendid villa of Mendip Lodge stood about two miles from Barley Wood. (This is completely untrue. Sarah Siddons had been a lifelong friend of Thomas Sedgwick Whalley, who was godfather to one of her daughters. Mrs Siddons and had long wanted to own a house in the same locality.) *This villa by the way was a show place in which a vast deal of money had been sunk, upon two follies of equally unproductive of pleasure to the beholder and of anything approaching a pecuniary compensation to the owner. The villa, with its embellishments, was supposed to have cost at least sixty thousand pounds, of which one half had been absorbed, partly by a contest with the natural obstacles of the situation, and partly by the frailest of all ornaments—vast china jars, vases and other 'knicknackery' baubles which held their very existence by so frail a tenure as the carefulness of a housemaid; and which at all events, if they should survive the accidents of life, never are known to reproduce to the possessor one-tenth part of what they have cost. Out of doors there are terraces of a mile long, one rising above another, and carried, by mere artifice of mechanic skill, along the perpendicular face of a lofty rock. Had they, when finished any particular beauty? Not at all. Considered as a pleasure ground, they formed a far less delightful landscape, and a far less alluring haunt to rambling steps, than most of the uncostly shrubberies which were seen below, in unpretending situations and upon the ordinary level of the vale. What a record of human imbecility! For all his pains and expense in forming this costly 'folly', his reward was daily anxiety, and one solitary bon mot which he used to record of some man, who on being asked what he thought of the house, replied, that 'He thought the Devil had tempted him up to an exceedingly high place'. No part of the grounds, nor the house itself, was at all the better because, originally, it has been beyond measure difficult to form it: so difficult that, according to Dr Johnson's witty remark, on another occasion, there was good reason for wishing that it had been impossible. The owner, whom I knew, most certainly never enjoyed a happy day in the costly creation;* (This again is completely untrue) *which, after all, displayed but little taste, though a gorgeous array of finery. The show part of the house was itself a monument to the barrenness of invention in him who planned it ; consisting, as it did of one long suite of rooms in a straight line, without variety without obvious parts, and therefore without symmetry or proportions.* (Again this is nonsense. Given the steepness of the site and bearing in mind the cost incurred in leveling enough space for a house to be built meant that the house had to be long and narrow.) *This long vista was so managed that, by means of folding doors, the whole could be seen at a glance, whilst its extent was magnified by a vast mirror at the further end.*[129]

For a full account of the house and garden, see Stephens, C.D., *The Reverend Dr Thomas Sedgwick Whalley and the Queen of Bath*. Candy Jar Books, Cardiff, 2014. Chapters 6 & 7.

Rear in the 1950s from the SE.

Bowling Green.

One of the two painted rooms.

The Dining Room.

The Drawing Room.

The Morning Room (The Bow Room).

The balcony.

The stables.

Further developments a) The West Harptree Turnpike 1793

At this time, coach travel between Bath and Mendip Lodge was not easy. One route was to take the turnpike from Bath to Bristol and then take the Bridgwater Turnpike to Churchill Cross (the present junction of the A38 and A368), from where it was only just over a mile, along the then unmade up road, to the entrance of Mendip Lodge. The turnpikes were good roads, but it meant a journey of 27 miles, which would have taken perhaps seven hours by coach. There were two alternatives which avoided going through Bristol. One was to take the Bath Turnpike Trust road (now the A39) as far as Hallatrow, where it met the Bristol Turnpike (A37), which soon became the Wells Trust Turnpike. After that, one had to cut across country for 12.5 miles along the north side of the Mendips, through West Harptree, Blagdon and Ubley, on an unmade up road, now the A368 but then no more than a track. Alternatively you could take the old Fosse Way, now the A367, but then still part of the Bath Turnpike Trust, as far as Stratton-on-the-Fosse but with this time 17 miles of unmade up road, which would have been hazardous, if not impassable, in the winter.

In light of this it is not surprising that the Whalley brothers, together with local landed friends and relatives such as Wickham, Hippisley Coxe, Tooker, and Popham, set out to sponsor an Act to build a West Harptree turnpike. This ran from the Bristol Bridgwater Turnpike at Churchill Cross, along the foot of the Mendips, to West Harptree and then turned north-east to connect with the Bristol to Wells Turnpike at Chelwood Bridge. The Act to construct this received its second reading in June, 1793.[130]

Notable also amongst the trustees of the new turnpike was Thomas Sedgwick's friend Henry Bosanquet, who was by then renting Langford Court, and John Hiley Addington, brother of the Prime Minister Lord Sidmouth, who, by 1797, had taken over the lease at Langford Court and would eventually buy the Langford estate in 1804.

Further developments b) The enclosure of the Churchill "wastelands"

Although agricultural enclosure was intended to be the means by which agricultural output was increased, it was often the case that it was used by local landowners to increase the size of their estates. Having now leased Langford Court and its surrounding estate, Thomas set about using this

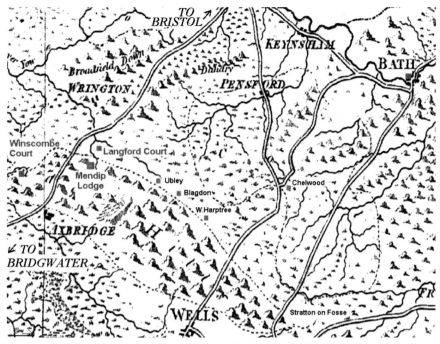

The state of the roads in 1792 and the route of the West Harptree turnpike after Billingsley 1795 (see text).

means to acquire adjacent land for Mendip Lodge. The Banwell and Churchill Enclosure Act of 1797 was one of nine awarded in the area.[131] This allowed the enclosure of much of the Mendip common land above Churchill. Thomas' brother, Francis Whalley, was one of the three commissioners appointed to implement its provisions. All those who had used the land were given rights to their own allocation but, as Billingsley states, this was, in reality, *"a little system of patronage"*.[132] As a result of his own allocation, and by buying up the holdings of others, Thomas Sedgwick Whalley was able to achieve a surrounding estate of almost 1,000 acres as well as improved road access to Mendip Lodge.

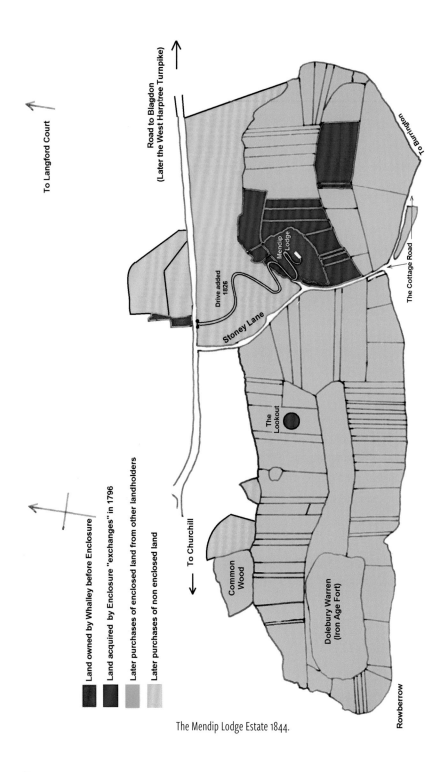

To Langford Court

Road to Blagdon
(Later the West Harptree Turnpike)

To Burrington

The Cottage Road

Drive added 1826

Mendip Lodge

Stoney Lane

The Lookout

To Churchill

Common Wood

Dolebury Warren
(Iron Age Fort)

Rowberrow

Land owned by Whalley before Enclosure

Land acquired by Enclosure "exchanges" in 1796

Later purchases of enclosed land from other landholders

Later purchases of non enclosed land

The Mendip Lodge Estate 1844.

FRANCES SAGE'S MARRIAGE

SHORTLY AFTER THE Whalleys returned from the continent in 1787, their 18-year-old niece Fanny Sage joined them in Bath for the winter season and was soon busy enjoying life there at her uncle's expense, but also to his delight. Her relationship with her uncle and aunt at this time was summarised in a later letter from Anna Seward to a friend, dated April, 1795:

Miss Sage was, in her infancy recommended to his care by the maternal tenderness of a beloved sister, expiring in the bloom of life. This sacred and precious trust Mr and Mrs Whalley executed with the most sedulous attention and fondest indulgence. She grew, she bloomed; the pride and delight of their hearts. Genius and wit aided, by rapidly acquired endowments, the fascinations of beauty. The creations of the pencil glow beneath her fingers. Her skill, taste and invention on the harpsichord is scare inferior to that of the first masters*; and to a voice of exquisite tone, power, compass and inflexion, she adds the touching graces of harmonic expression, in a degree of excellence that approaches to enchantment. She was abroad with the aunt and uncle Whalley in the year 1786 and, mistress of French and Italian, she conversed, sung, she played, she danced, the day-star of our island; so that nothing was more talked of in the then happy French cities than the charming English woman.[133]

* i.e a professional. There were two other similar but independent reports of her playing. [134, 135]

She was, by now, known as the *Queen of Bath* for her good looks, witty conversation, her singing and her playing of the harpsichord and guitar.

Lowndes records that, in 1939, there remained a notice in one of the rooms of 20 Royal Crescent, then occupied by the British Boxboard Agency, bearing the inscription *'Fanny Sage known for her beauty as the Queen of Bath lived here in 1787'.*[136] She was not the first to hold this unofficial title; the first was being Juliana Popjoy, mistress of Beau Nash, who was Master of the Ceremonies at Bath. Later contenders are fully explored by White,[137] but by May, 1789, the 19-year-old Frances had assumed the title and was clearly having a wonderful time as the centre of attraction in Bath. However, this was causing Thomas' cousin, Sophia Weston, some anxiety:

> *Has our lovely Fanny made any new conquests and may I dare to drop a hint that I wish you would not let her run so much about Bath in a morning? Walking is certainly good for her health, and necessary; but the misfortune of Bath is that young people cannot take the advantage of exercise without being too much exposed to observation. Fanny is too attractive not to be much sought after, but she should not be too easily or too frequently found. When you and Mrs Whalley think she is walking in the Crescent, she is often flying all over the Parades. The dear thing is wonderfully prone to flirtation, and hunts after a new beau, who has happened to strike her fancy, with a degree of activity and interest more natural than fit. I am sorry to say that her cousin, Miss Wickham, seemed much more inclined to lead her into this sort of thing than, as she ought, to be a check upon her. Miss King is also intolerably giddy. Perhaps the indulgence of always having a young friend to run about with her, may be ultimately of the most serious disadvantage to Fanny. Be assured, though I heard many remarks upon this subject, I have not ventured to speak from the observation of others. Fanny loves me, and my time of life is not formidable to her. I had, therefore, ample means of making my own observations, such as even yourself or Mrs Whalley could not have.*
>
> *I know how delicate interference of this sort is amongst friends; but I also know that I am influenced only by motives of the purest attachment to Fanny's interest, and I know moreover the candour and liberality of my dear cousin Thomas. Therefore however ill judged these remarks may appear, I have no fear in submitting them to your indulgence.*[138]

'A view of the Parades at Bath' attributed to Humphrey Repton. Copyright *Bath in Time.*

Miss Wickham *'who should have known better'* was probably the 26-year-old Elizabeth Mary Wickham (1763-1823), her cousin who, perhaps significantly, like other former Queens of Bath, was to remain a spinster. The 'Miss King' referred to could perhaps have been a daughter of James King, Master of the Ceremonies (1744-1816), who is mentioned in Jane Austin's Northanger Abbey.

The cartoon above, which is attributed to Humphrey Repton, gives a clear illustration of what Miss Weston was concerned about. Indeed, the young lady in the centre of the picture bears a striking resemblance to the painting of the 16-year-old Frances. Repton was a member of the Anna Seward circle and at this time was attempting to establish himself as a garden designer.[139] He would later design several in the Bristol area, notably that of Blaise Castle (1796) for Whalley's friend John Harford, the wealthy Bristol merchant and banker. Repton was also an excellent artist and Anna Seward, in a letter to him in February, 1786, says: *'You tell me Mrs Repton reads to you in an evening while you draw'*.[140] Seward had a high regard for Repton and made a point of introducing him to Thomas Sedgwick in a letter of October, 1788:

I should suppose that nobody has ever been so well qualified as yourself for

the profession you purpose (sic) to assume, that of landscape gardener;...
Mr Whalley will be in Bath this Winter, he is very warm hearted and oratorically
persuasive and I have interested him in your fame and success. [141]

At that time, Thomas Sedgwick was very much engaged in building and laying out the gardens for his 'cottage' at Langford,[142] and if Repton took up the offer of this introduction he may well have met Frances, as the Whalleys were in residence at Royal Crescent by the following January.

Perhaps as a result of Miss Weston's concern, Frances was married a year later to an Irishman, William Townsend Mullins, an heir to a large fortune. She was now 20-years-old, but he was 29 and already a widower. His first wife had died in 1788,[143] and his two daughters, Anna (b.1785) and Elizabeth (b.1786), would spend all their lives in Ireland.

William had been educated in Limerick at the School of the Reverend Daniel Monsell and then entered Trinity College Dublin in June, 1779, where, as *Socius Comitatus* (a Fellow Commoner), he paid double fees in order to graduate in three years rather than the usual four.[144] How he and Frances met, or how the marriage was arranged, is not known. The Mullins family seat was Burnham House, County Kerry in Ireland, and his father, who was to become the first Lord Ventry, was immensely wealthy and so William must have seemed a good prospect for a husband. The marriage settlement of £17,000, equivalent to £1.5m today, was paid jointly by Isaac Sage, Thomas Sedgwick Whalley and his wife. Such a dowry was intended, through investment by her husband, to provide £1,000 per annum for Frances in the event of his death.[145]

Yet the choice of such a husband was a surprising one for the beautiful and talented Frances Sage. Certainly William Mullins' father was extremely wealthy but he did not yet have a title, though would become a baronet in 1795 and Baron Ventry in 1800. But where were all the young dashing, and unmarried titled gentlemen who had come to Bath to find such a beauty as Frances? Could it be perhaps that Frances was already a woman with a reputation? Maybe the epithet '*Queen of Bath*' carried with it a warning to polite society. Kitty Fisher, who held the title from 1760-1767, never married; neither did Miss Susannah Wroughton, who held the title for the next 10 years. Mrs Alicia Macartney, Frances' immediate predecessor in the role, only achieved the title after the death of her her husband. Her reputation was well known,[146] and her time at 30 Royal Crescent overlapped that of the Whalleys at number 20. Fanny Burney, that acute observer of 18th century life, was in no doubt as to her character:

Mrs Alicia (Bad Mac) MacCartney, my godmother Frances Greville's eldest sister, was a notorious drunkard, an assistant to the vices of others and as infamous a practicer of all species of them herself. She was one of the worst women breathing but even this notorious woman contrived to get company to her mansion and to be countenanced by people of character and rank by keeping a superb house and giving the most elegant entertainments.[147]

By this time, sensuality had become the antonym of respectability,[148] and Miss Weston's remarks about Frances and her cousin allude to a dangerous disregard for propriety. In this context it is perhaps also significant that her cousin, Elizabeth Mary Wickham, who appears to have led Frances into compromising situations, also never married.

However, that said, according to Anna Seward:

Mr Mullins (was) a gentleman of graceful person, splendid fortune and generous virtues, the impassioned choice of her (Frances Sage's) avowed intentions.[149]

William Mullins and Frances Sage were married on 12th May, 1790, in Walcot Parish Church, Bath.[150,151] It is to be assumed that one or more of her three uncles were in attendance and perhaps their mother too, who, although in her 84th year, was still to live for another 10 years. The marriage was not conducted by either of her ordained uncles but by the Rector of St Swithin's Walcot, John Sibley. Romney painted a full-length portrait of Frances at about this time; sadly, the whereabouts of this remains unknown. There exists another portrait attributed to him of '*Lady in a white dress*' which might well be of Frances; both her facial appearance, the position of the head and the sheet of the music in her hand bear a striking similarity to the earlier painting by Cosway.

Frances Sage, aged 16, and "Lady in a White Dress", attributed to George Romney.

Six months into the marriage, Thomas Sedgwick thought that all was well and had communicated his contentment to his friend Anna Seward, who replied in December 1790:

> I am glad... that the temper and disposition of him to whom your darling niece has given her herself, is so amiable.[152]

After their marriage the couple, and Frances' father Isaac Sage, went to Ireland to meet the Mullins family. According to Isaac Sage's valet, James Daxon, they stayed at the house of William Mullins' father at *'Tarbutt in the County of Kerry'*.[153] This could not have been Tarbot House, near Killarney, as this was then in the ownership of the Leslie family, but would have been Piermount House, Tarbert, on the shores of the River Shannon and William's family home. This was still being lived in by a members of the Mullins family as recently as 1944. One can only imagine the shock which the prospect of a future lived on the West Coast of Ireland made on Frances, who was used to the refinement, elegance and social whirl of Bath, and she never again visited Ireland, though William returned several times to see his father, quite possibly to plead for money with which to buy a house in England.

According to Porter, the married lady in polite 18th century society had four functions:[154] to obey her husband, produce heirs, run the household and be ladylike. She became *'mistress of the family'* and her domain and pride was the family home. Her role, as a dignified efficient housekeeper and mother, was a source of personal satisfaction and public esteem and her husband was expected to honour his wife's authority on all domestic matters.[155]

Frances would have expected that her husband, who was due to inherit his father's title and income of £32,000 a year (i.e £2.7m at today's value),[156] would now be given money by his father to buy a house in England. However, as Thomas Sedgwick was to discover, William's father was "an avaricious and a mean skinflint". He was also exceptionally long lived, with the result that William did not inherit until just two years before his own death, in 1827, which meant that Frances and William Mullins were far less well off than her father and Thomas Sedgwick might have imagined when the marriage was arranged.[157]

Three years after they were married, Frances still had no house and had produced no child. To make matters worse, William *"hated balls, assemblies, suppers and late hours"*, all of which had been a major features of Frances' life before she was married.

CHAPTER 7

FRANCES' DIVORCE

BY 1793, IT had become clear to Frances' close friends that all was not well in her marriage. In October of that year, Mrs Siddons had written to Thomas Sedgwick saying how sad she was to learn of Frances' *'unhappy situation'* and hoping her beautiful hands will soon be fully restored.[158] Quite whether the unhappy situation referred to her hands, or the unhappy marriage, is not clear. Was this perhaps a psychosomatic skin disorder or had Frances self-harmed? Two months later, in December, 1793, Frances received a letter from Princess D'Arenberg, who was of similar age and with whom she had formed a close friendship when they met in 1786. (See Chapter 5 and Appendix 3). In this letter, the Princess mentions that William might be going to the continent to join the war with France and suggests:

If Mr Mullins crosses the sea for the sake of military glory you should for his sake come nearer the centre of military operation; and why would you not stay in Brussels where you have left many friends and certainly you would hear more frequently news of your husband.... [159, 160]

By April, 1795, there was wider knowledge of the breakdown of the Mullins' marriage, though this appears to be confined to close friends. Thomas and his wife had visited their trusted friend Anna Seward in March of that year and in the latter's letter to Mrs Powys dated 1st April we learn that the breakdown was of longstanding, starting only a year after their marriage:

After a twelve month's ardent attention to him, repaid on his part by the most devoted indulgence, she grew cold, apparently oppressed by every instance of his regard, and charmed by the admiration of other men. She racked his heart with jealousy, and received his expostulations with scorn; grieved and alarmed from time to time by her levities, those tender friends who had been the guardians of her youth (The Whalleys); and at last, a few month since, eloped with Captain Tothe (sic: clearly an error) of the Guards, with whom she now lives in total disgrace, reckless of having blasted her constellation of talents- reckless of this dire apostacy from gratitude, from love, from honour, and from duty. [161]

Despite having good reason to divorce his wife, it is clear from the deposition made to the Consistory Court by her maid, Mara Brazier, that it was Frances who had determined to leave her husband.[162] At that time there were only three options in such a situation: mutual acceptance of leading separate lives, legal separation, or divorce. As the need for a male heir must have been the main reason for William's second marriage (as it was his later third marriage), he must have realised that the only way out for him was divorce by Act of Parliament, since a legal separation would not permit him to remarry.

Separation and Divorce in the Eighteenth Century

Before the Matrimonial Causes Act of 1857, which set up special courts to deal with divorce, the only way to obtain a divorce was by a private Act of Parliament. Before 1700, even this was not possible. Between 1700 and 1857, there were about 350 Divorce Acts passed in the House of Lords. Divorce was granted only for adultery. Women could not obtain a divorce from their husbands unless the adultery was compounded with other offences, such as bigamy or incest. In reality, divorce was invariably given to men, there being only four Divorce Acts granted to women before 1857.[163]

Before the House of Lords would consider an Act for divorce, it required a court order for separation, confusingly called divorce '*a mensa et thoro*' (not allowing remarriage), from an ecclesiastical court, together with a verdict of '*criminal conversation*', that is adultery. The procedure of the Bishop's Consistory Court was very different from the civil court system of today. The parties to a case provided witnesses to attempt to persuade the court of their case (or defence). These witnesses were known as deponents, as their evidence was given by deposition: that is, a sworn written statement of the facts in response to a written list of questions (called interrogatories) drawn up in advance. The court required these to be from at least seven independent witnesses.[164] Once the court verdict of criminal conversation had been achieved, the husband could then petition the King for a Divorce Act and, if granted, the House of Lords re-heard the case to ensure that adultery was proven and that there had been no connivance, collusion or condonation by the husband.[165] Such trials were held in public.

While divorce was not confined to the nobility and landed gentry, most cases were as it usually concerned the matter of inheritance and was not a cheap undertaking. The estimates are that the overall cost of a divorce might be £70,000 at today's prices, excluding damages which could be sought. Legal costs were not borne by the plaintiff but by the adulterer and damages awarded to men who brought successful cases against their wives were usually high. The Mullins' divorce, though, is the only one recorded between an heir to a title and his wife before 1800.

The Divorce

What happened in January, 1795, is recounted through the various depositions presented to the Ecclesiastical Court.[162] These had been taken during May and early June, 1795. It seems that on January 26th, Frances and her husband were planning to leave Osborns Hotel in London to visit the Whalleys at Langford. Under the pretence that she would go via her uncle, Joseph Sage, who lived at Reading, Frances, accompanied only by her maid, left alone. Having set out Frances then told her maid, Mara Brazier, that she and her husband were about to part and she would not be going to Langford, but would lodge somewhere where she could not be found. Having failed to find suitable lodgings in Piccadilly, she directed the coach to Kensington Gravel Pits (about where Notting Hill Gate now is) and stopped at what the maid thought was a friend's house for the night. As will be recounted later, this was probably a brothel. Soon after she arrived, Frances wrote a letter which she sent out and, later that evening, Captain Abel Rous Dottin, of the Life Guards, arrived and stayed talking to Frances until 10 or 11 o'clock.

The Kensington Gravel Pits where Frances Sage lodged on the night of January, 26th, 1795.

The following morning her husband and father arrived and talked with Frances for some while, but then departed. Two hours later, her father returned in his carriage and took Frances and her maid back to his house in Albemarle Street. There Frances stayed, until the 30th when she ordered a sedan chair which took her to the coach stand in Oxford Street, from where she took a Hackney Coach to the Castle Inn at Richmond. There she met and stayed with Captain Dottin, acting as man and wife. When Mr Sage and Mr Mullins arrived the following evening, the innkeeper (who was well known to Dottin) at first denied that the couple had shared a room but was later told by Captain Dottin to tell the truth. Mr Sage and Mr Mullins then departed but the couple stayed for a further three days before leaving to stay at the Grassiers Hotel in Jermyn Street, where they registered as Mr and Mrs Dottin. This was clearly more convenient since it was exactly midway between Frances' father's house in Albemarle Street and Dottin's barracks. The maid was summoned from

Albemarle Street to attend her mistress for several days thereafter, which must have been with the agreement of Isaac Sage, to whose house she had returned on the 27th. The couple then moved to lodgings in Grosvenor Square and finally lodgings at 6 Brook Street; these various locations ensuring that there would be enough reliable independent witnesses who could provide statements of 'criminal conversation' between the couple.

Some four months after Frances left her husband, but before the hearing in the Consistory Court took place, her maid Maria Brazier was in the service of the Reverend George Markham, soon to become Dean of York, and it was from here that she wrote her deposition on 2nd May, 1795. Maria was the only weak link in what appears to have been the carefully arranged scheme. She must have overheard much of the planning so it was better that she was out of the way as soon as possible. The divorce became public knowledge at the end of July, 1795, when the Bath Gazette and Weekly Advertiser, the Ipswich Journal and The Times all contained reports of the hearing on Tuesday, 21st July, when Consistory Court of the Bishop of London had found Frances guilty of adultery with Captain Dottin of the Guards.[166,167,168]

Following the findings of the Consistory Court, William Mullins obtained the remarkably low damages of £500 with costs against Dottin in the Court of the Kings Bench.[169] Mullins was now free to petition the King to bring about an Act of Divorce. The first reading of this was held on 3rd December 1795 and the second reading on 4th February, 1796. The Bill was then considered by a Committee of the House of Lords on 18th February, and finally was made effective from March, 1796.[170]

Who was Captain Abel Rous Dottin?

Abel Rouse Dottin was the same age as Frances, and the eldest son of very wealthy parents. Though Abel and his brother were born in London, both sides of his family were plantation owners in Barbados,[171] and had been for several generations, but their parents married and lived in England. Abel Dottin senior went on to become High Sheriff of Oxford. The Dottin family had a London house as well as a substantial house in Princes Buildings, Bath, which was described as having a double staircase, a large garden, a coach house containing a post coach and two phaetons, and stabling for four horses.[172]

Princes Street and Royal Crescent were only a few hundred yards apart and the Dottins' must have attended the same church in Walcot as the Whalleys and Frances Sage when she was in Bath. The Dottin boys attended a boarding school in Bristol. Both Abel, his father and grandfather were Oxford graduates and Abel attended Queen's College.

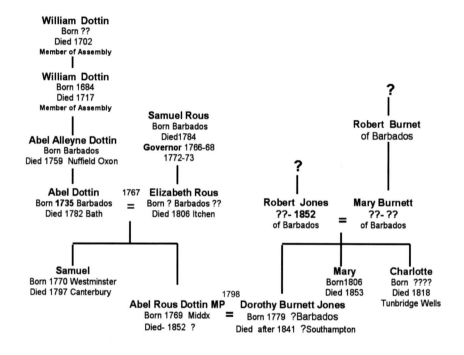

The Dottin family tree.

Because Frances and he were of the same age, and because his father had a house in Bath, they must have known each other in their teens, especially as Abel was known for his *'good minuet'*. By the time of the divorce, Able Dottin was 26-years-old, and had risen to the rank of Captain in the 2nd Life Guards, so it is likely that he entered the army directly after leaving university. This would have removed him from the Bath social scene before Frances reached an age to contemplate marriage, but they could still have met at social functions when he was on leave.

By 1790, Abel was based at St. James Palace barracks at the bottom of Albermarle Street. This was only a few hundred yards from the Sage's final

'Loyal Souls – the Mess Room at St. James Capt Abel Rous Dottin proposes the loyal toast
© National Portrait Gallery, London.

house, and on the direct route between the Officers Mess and Dottin's own house in Argyle Street. So this is perhaps how they met again in London, or maybe at a concert in the nearby Hanover Square Rooms.

While the witness statements and picture of the Officers Mess at St James paint a picture of Captain Dottin as a typical 18th century rake, there is a much more flattering engraving made by H.B.Hall of a painting by Sir Thomas Lawrence. Lawrence was a lifelong friend of Dottin from the time when, in 1782, as a precocious 13-year-old Lawrence had sketched Abel and his brother in Bath.[173,174] Although the later engraving is entitled *'Abel Rous Dottin MP'* the subject looks to be no more than 25 years of age, and about the time of his entanglement with Frances. Since Dottin didn't become MP until the age of 49, the portrait by his friend Lawrence must have been undertaken much earlier.

The Divorce Act provided for a generous settlement to Frances of £1,000 per year for life. This sum was derived from the income arising from her dowry, which had been provided by her father and Thomas Whalley and his wife, which remained the property of her former husband. This income would

Abel Rous Dottin
The engraving by HB Hall of the painting by
Sir Thomas Lawrence, published in 1830.

have been enough to keep a single woman in modest comfort. In *Sense and Sensibility*, written by Jane Austen only a few years after Frances' marriage, there is a conversation between Marianne and Elinor during which Marianne considers a suitable income for setting up house:

And yet two thousand a-year is a very moderate income, said Marianne. A family cannot well be maintained on a smaller. I am sure I am not extravagant in my demands. A proper establishment of servants, a carriage, perhaps two, and hunters, cannot be supported on less.

Very surprisingly, all parties remained on very good terms after the divorce, strongly suggesting careful planning. Had the Consistory Court discovered this, the divorce would have been denied. William Mullins still had no male heir and was now free to remarry. This he did 18 months later, in September, 1797.[175] He and Thomas Sedgwick Whalley remained on the closest terms and Thomas seems to have lent a large sum of money to William against the day when he would inherit from his father.[176] Twenty years later, in November, 1815, Thomas visited William and his family in Brussels and stayed there for several months. In his correspondence at that time to his lifelong friend, Arthur Anstey, he speaks in the warmest terms of both William, who he describes as *'my old and steady friend'*, and *'the lovely and amiable'* third Mrs Mullins and their son.[177, 178]

What happened to Captain Abel Rous Dottin?

Being cited in the divorce did not hold Captain Dottin back. Three years later, in March, 1798, he married Dorothy Burnett Jones, from another extremely wealthy West Indies family. Her father had been Attorney General of Barbados and her sister would become Lady Arundel.[179]

Dottin's means of election to parliament in 1818 adds further weight, if any were needed, to the idea that Frances' divorce was engineered with the agreement of all parties, for he achieved his seat with the help of Frances' father, Isaac Sage, via the Constituency of Gatton, near Reigate in Surrey. Isaac Sage, having sold Thornhill, had been living at Gatton Park, a fine Palladian mansion since sometime before 1811, when he rewrote his will as '*Isaac Sage of Gatton*'. It would seem he was renting the estate from Sir Mark Wood, who had been created baronet in 1808. Both had been members of the East India Company until its dissolution in 1818 and both were keen race goers. Sir Mark had been a colonel in the East India Company and had become its Chief Engineer in Bengal when Isaac had been Governor of Patna in West Bengal, so perhaps their friendship was of long standing.

Gatton was possibly the most rotten of all rotten boroughs at the time. The village had 23 houses, of which perhaps as few as six were within the borough, so electors were never more than a handful, of which the most important was the Lord of the Manor, living at Gatton Park, to whom it was pointless to stand in opposition. A delightful account of the election of 1816, just two years before Dottin's election there, is recorded by Henry Stook Smith, who describes the circumstances which are likely to have pertained for Dottin. It appears that, in 1816, there were uniquely two candidates for the one vacant seat and in the event, Mr Wood the younger defeated a Mr Jennings by one vote. However:

> *Mr Jennings was Sir Mark Wood's butler and there were only three voters Sir Mark, his son and Jennings. The son was away and Jennings and his master quarrelled, upon which Jennings refused to second the son and proposed himself. To get a seconder for his son Sir Mark had to second Jennings, and it was ultimately arranged, and the vote of Sir Mark alone given. This was the only contest within memory.* [180]

Sir Mark's London House in Pall Mall was only half a mile from Isaac's house in Albemarle Street. Thus, even if Isaac had not been acting as the Lord of the Manor of Gatton himself in 1818, he clearly had it in his power to ask Sir Mark to ensure Abel Rous Dottin's election.

In the subsequent election of 1826, Dottin became MP for Southampton and was thereafter a pillar of Southampton society. He became a JP and later High Sheriff of the County but does not seem to have been a particularly active MP, though he notably chaired the committee which proposed the establishment of the Southampton Docks Railway. He retired from parliament in 1841.

What happened to Frances Mullins (née Sage)

In July, 1795, only a few days after the hearing at the Court of the Kings bench became public, Mrs Piozzi's daughter Cecilia (to whom Thomas Whalley was godfather) was referring to Frances as *'that dreadful Mrs Mullins'*. She even suggests, in her letter dated 2nd July, that the death of Thomas Sedgwick's first wife had been brought about by the distress which Frances had caused her aunt.[181] This was wholly incorrect, since the first Mrs Whalley did not die until 8th December, 1801, but the Whalley's close friend Anna Seward reported that they were *'both ill, distracted and depressed this time'*,[182] although six months later she also reported finding them *'well and cheerful'*![183]

Some weeks earlier Mrs Piozzi had pressed her close friend Penelope Pennington for details of Mrs Mullins' disgrace. It is clear that she never had a high opinion of her.[184] Penelope, who as Sophie Weston before her marriage had in earlier days, regarded herself as a friend and confidant of Frances Sage. Now she replies in unusually severe terms:

After alarming and teizing her Friends with great Impropriety of conduct for above these two years past; (her) Husband was about two Months since too well convinced, that he had still more to complain of. Think however of her Depravity, when in the same Week that she confessed to a Criminal Connexion with One Man, and was pardoned (sic) on fair promises of better things, She commenced an intrigue with another! no less a Person than the Dancing Mr Dottin, who you must recollect at Bath – famous for his Debaucheries and Good Minuet – On the discovery of which poor Mullins immediately carried her to her father in London,- from which she eloped twice in one week, -Once they traced her to a House of no good Fame in Kensington and the second time to the Castle at Richmond, where she had been two days and two nights with Dottin - passing for his wife - and when her Father in tears and agony requested, that she would not let him leave her in a Brothel; she treated him with the utmost Contempt, - did every thing but laugh in his Face, and refusing to return with him, remained there with her Paramour, with whom she continues in London where her Husband is preparing, with Mr Erskine's assistance, to obtain such redress as the Law will afford him. [185]

One interpretation of such a description was that Frances had, by this time, become a high class prostitute; another that she was desperately bored with her husband and her peripatetic lifestyle and was pursuing the only way out available to her.

With a divorce settlement of £1,000 per year from William Mullins, there was no real reason for her to remarry.[186] Yet, on 26th March, 1796, only three weeks after the Divorce Act had its third reading, Frances married another Irishman, the Reverend Robert Boyle Sullivan, in Westminster.[187]

The marriage of the divorced Frances Mullins to Robert Boyle Sullivan, Marylebone, Westminster, March 1796.

This was by special licence rather than the cheaper option of having the banns read, which eliminated the risk that an objection might be voiced! The officiating clergyman, the Reverend Benjamin Lawrence (B.A. Oxon, 1782), is described in the Oxford University Alumni (1500-1886) as a gentleman of Builth Wells, who had been recently ordained in Lincoln in 1795. He became Curate of St Mary's Marylebone in 1798, although he was later (a largely absentee) Rector of Carsington.[188] It is quite possible that he was unaware that Frances had been married and divorced, since she is recorded in the licence as being a spinster, nor that the groom was a member of the clergy, as he signed himself as '*Boyle Sullivan*'. It is, of course, true that many Irishmen dropped the 'O' on coming to England but why exclude his Christian name in a Christian marriage register?

Was this a second marriage of love, or one of convenience to enable Frances to continue to live the life of a courtesan? In either case, at this time she could not risk having her future husband cited as the co-respondent. Technically, divorce was granted to the plaintiff, allowing him or her to remarry; such permission was not given to the guilty party, but in reality there was no way in which the law could prevent this from happening. However, at the time, efforts were being made in the House of Lords to change the law so that a guilty woman could not marry her paramour! While this failed to become law, at the time it must have been seen as a real threat. So, what Frances and her husband-to-be needed was someone they could trust to play the part of adulterer without putting Frances too much at risk. Abel Rous Dottin, who already had a reputation for "debauchery", was an ideal choice.

Who was the Reverend Robert Boyle Sullivan?

Many Irish moving to England in the 18th century would drop the 'O' from their surnames. The Database of the Clergy of the Church of England first records a Robert Sullivan on 5th August, 1806, as being licensed on that date as the curate of St. James the Great, Winscombe.[189] As this appointment was made by was by Bishop Beadon, and Winscombe Court was now occupied by Francis Whalley, this was yet another example of Thomas Sedgwick's influence. Bishop Beadon and Thomas Sedgwick were related through their mothers,[190] and it is clear from earlier correspondence that they were very good friends, and also that the Bishop knew Frances.[191]

Most unusually, the Database of the Clergy of the Church of England gives nothing of Robert Sullivan's early life. His BA degree is not recorded at a British university, nor does his name occur in the Alumni Dublinenses.[192] However, a Robert Boyle O'Sullivan appears in the '*Catalogue of Graduates of Dublin University*' as obtaining a BA in 1782.[193] This would make him about the same age as Frances Sage. The Boyles and O'Sullivans were prominent families in County Cork at the time. (The Anglo-Irish politician Richard Boyle was created 1st Earl of Cork in 1620). There is a Reverend Boyle O 'Sullivan listed by the Cork Historical and Archaeological Society as being in Cork in 1788 and the Clerical and Parochial Records of Cloyne, Cork and Ross identify a Boyle Sullivan as being appointed a Deacon of Cork in September 1783, which would have been the year after Robert Boyle O'Sullivan's graduation.[194]

Sophia Louisa Egerton, a witness at the wedding, appears to be related to Francis Sutherland Egerton 1st Earl of Ellesmere. Francis Egerton had links with the Boyles and a poem ascribed to him is about Boyle Farm, a mansion in Thames Ditton and home of Charlotte Boyle Walsingham.[195] The Sullivan Baronets also lived at Thames Ditton, notably Sir Richard Joseph Sullivan 1st Baronet, who had been born in Dublin in 1752. This all suggests strong family links between the Boyles, Sullivans and Egertons.

How did Frances Sage and Robert Sullivan meet?

Frances Sullivan's Will of November, 1850, indicates that Major General John Stafford had married her close friend and cousin, Frances Maria Whalley, daughter of Francis Whalley, as *'the nephew of my late husband Robert Boyle Sullivan'*. Hill Wickham also refers to Robert Boyle Sullivan as a relative of General Stafford.[196] Further investigations have shown that Robert's sister, Thomasine Sullivan, married Hugh Stafford in Cork in 1780. (Her father was Rev H. Sullivan, of Clonakilty, Co. Cork, from which it might be assumed that their mother was a Boyle.) The Staffords must have soon moved to Somerset as their son, John Stafford, was born in Winscombe in 1785, and thus the family became neighbours of Francis Edwards Whalley and his family at Winscombe Court.

The effect of the Divorce on the Whalleys

It seems almost certain that the divorce was carefully stage-managed by Frances, her father and William Mullins, and that Thomas Whalley and his wife were certainly aware of the couple's estrangement; correspondence also suggests that they were devastated by the divorce. Anna Seward, writing to her friends Mrs Powys one month after Frances had left Mr Mullins, states:

The 13th of March brought Mr and Mrs Whalley to me, whose dear society I have also very recently lost. One of the heaviest afflictions that can wring the feeling bosom, after having tormented them near two years with terror of this descent, became, some four months since, complete: an affliction, the corrosive bitterness of which must inevitably mingle with all of comfort which they may hereafter taste, till human evil, neither by immediate pressure, nor cruel recollection, may annoy them more. [197]

Their friends were horrified at Frances' defection; some of the more straight-laced thereafter avoided any further contact with the Whalleys,[198] and by their own choice the Whalleys cut themselves off from their close friends for many weeks after the divorce.[199] It would seem, though, that Frances continued her contact with Thomas and his wife as, one year later, in October, 1797, Anna Seward, writing to Thomas Sedgwick, expresses her sympathy at some new indiscretion, and hoped that '*her* (Frances) *new dereliction will for the present prevent the repetition of those letters of hers which must torture you to no purpose*'.[200] Quite what the new dereliction was, or what the earlier letters from Frances were asking, is not clear; perhaps Frances was asking for money (see below).

Life of the Sullivans after their marriage

Mrs Piozzi seems to have shared her daughter's low opinion of Frances. A letter from her (formerly Mrs Thrale, née Hester Lynch, who was one of Thomas Sedgwick's lifelong correspondents) to Sophia Pennington, née Weston, dated April 4th, 1799, suggests that, despite Frances' £,1000pa divorce settlement, the couple were soon short of money:

His unfortunate niece, cydevant [+] *Fanny Sage sent to me yesterday for £20; and said she was detained (for debt I trow) at our poor petty town of St Asaph two miles off. A tall ill looking man on horseback brought the letter but will not, I hope revenge my refusal of his lady's request, when Dumouriez shall have set all the wild Irish at full liberty.* I was half afraid, sure enough, yet little disposed to give what would make 40 honest cottagers happy for a gay lass (she was just 30 years old) who I never liked in her best days, and who never had any claims on my friendship which she now talks so loudly of.* [201]

+A misspelling of ci-devant, a derogatory comment from the French, meaning "from before" and technically applied to members of the French nobility.

*A reference to the French General Charles-François Dumouriez who was thought to be about to bring Ireland in to the War on the side of Napoleon, providing confirmation that the messenger was Irish – clearly Frances husband Robert Boyle Sullivan!

It is clear that, at this time, she had never met the Reverend Boyle Sullivan but later that year, in July, 1799, she was aware of the couple's relationship, for she wrote to Sophia Pennington:

Mr and Mrs Sullivan certainly were in this Neighbourhood together, whether they have parted since or not; and they had a niece of his with them, and they were much liked at St. Asaph till People found out who and what they were. He was said to be a Clergyman – Is he in orders or no? Sure Fanny Sage's Life must be beyond all Novels ever written. When will she finish her mad Career? People hereabouts admired her Accomplishments, but said there was very little Beauty to boast.[202]

Perhaps her dislike for Frances Sage stemmed from the early days of the latter's marriage to William Mullins, when Frances had ignored her in London. Clearly this affront upset Mrs Piozzi enough for her to relate the matter to her friend Anna Seward who, in turn, relayed it to Thomas Sedgwick.[203] Since Mrs Piozzi was hugely rich by her first husband's fortune, she would normally have regarded £20 as of little consequence when dealing with a friend, which is perhaps why Frances sought her out.

The next mention of Frances occurs in a letter that Hill Wickham quotes in connection with the '*Blagdon Controversy*' which was raging at this time.[204] This is given the date of June, 1802, and we are told that Mrs Sullivan was then living in '*Sydcot*' not far from Winscombe. In October, 1803, three years before he was appointed Curate of Winscombe, the London Gazette recorded that the Reverend Boyle Sullivan had been appointed Chaplain to the Western Regiment of the Mendip Legion, a volunteer regiment whose Commandant, appointed the same year, was Thomas' elder brother, and Frances' uncle, Lieutenant Colonel Francis Edwards Whalley, of Winscombe Court.[205] Since Francis Edward's daughter, Frances Maria Whalley, and Frances Sullivan had

St. James the Great, Winscombe where Rev Robert Boyle Sullivan was curate (1806-1810).

long been close friends, and were living close by, the appointment was perhaps inevitable.

Two years later, in June, 1808, Frances Maria Whalley married Major John Stafford at the same church. His uncle, the Curate Robert Boyle Sullivan (now of course married to her cousin Frances), is recorded as being a witness. However, Robert was only to remain as curate at Winscombe from 1806-1810, as he was removed from office in 1811 for neglecting his duties.[206] Notwithstanding this, in 1814 Robert was appointed as Stipendiary Curate at Bradford-on-Avon at the Chapel of Stoke (Limpley Stoke), a few miles south of Bath. How this came about is not known but one suspects again that Thomas Sedgwick was instrumental. Such an appointment was only possible because Bradford-on-Avon came within the diocese of Salisbury, and so Robert Sullivan's earlier dereliction of duties would have been unknown or could have been glossed over! This new appointment carried a stipend of £60 plus "surplice fees of Stoke". Robert was *directed to reside at Holt, 3 miles away, the Vicarage house being occupied by Mr Knight, resident curate of Bradford, to whom Sullivan is assistant'*. Sadly, while his surname is recorded, no details exist in the Church of England Database about Knight, not even his Christian name.

How long Robert Sullivan held the curacy in Bradford-on-Avon is also unknown, but soon the couple would join those Britons who flocked to France, as they had done after the Treaty of Amiens in 1802. Removal to France was not possible until the signing of the second Peace of Paris in 1816 but, by 1820, and perhaps a few years earlier, the Sullivans were living at La Fléche, to be visited by their uncle in May of that year.[207]

Maybe it had always been the Sullivans' wish to live in France, where they could live more cheaply and Frances would no longer have to endure the social estrangement of Bath, which an unfaithful divorcee attracted at this time. The fact that the Sullivans and the Staffords moved at about the same time, and the latter lived only 50 km away in Saumur, Sarthe, might suggest that the two Whalley cousins planned their removal together. By this time, Colonel Francis Whalley had died (1813), as had Frances Sullivan's father Isaac Sage (1818), so there were no close family ties to keep them in England. Unlike Frances, her close friend Frances Maria Stafford (née Whalley) raised a large family.[208] Their youngest son was born there in August, 1828, shortly after Robert Boyle Sullivan's death. Perhaps as a consequence, he was named Boyle Torriano Stafford.[209]

THE SECOND MRS WHALLEY

W E KNOW LITTLE of the character of Thomas' first wife, Elizabeth, apart from the poem he had written on the first anniversary of their wedding (See Appendix 1), and from comments recorded by Anna Seward in September, 1788:

> *She is a pleasing rational companion, infinitely estimable, though genius may not have infused her ideas, as those of her husband, in its ethereal dyes* (sic).[210]

In early April, 1789, two years after the Whalleys returned from France, Mrs Whalley had been thrown from her "whisky" (a light, covered, two-wheeled carriage for two persons, drawn by a single horse) into Langford Brook.[211] According to Hill Wickham, her spine was injured and *'her body became much bent'*. She recovered only slowly and partially but nonetheless maintained her usual cheerfulness for the next 11 years.[212] On the face of it, her sudden and unexpected death at the Cottage on December 8th, 1801, caused Thomas Sedgwick less suffering than would that of his second wife or of his mother. There is no mention of his feelings of remorse in any of his correspondence at this time, which is entirely out of character for someone who had written so affectionately of his wife on the first anniversary of their wedding.[213] It is highly likely that his biographer Hill Wickham omitted such letters from the two volumes of his great uncle's correspondence.

Thomas' true feelings are implied by Anna Seward in a letter she wrote to him two years later, after the death of her close friend John Saville, vicar choral of Lichfield. She says:

I had always understood, my kind friend, that, from the first of your loss in the close of the year 1801, you had resisted all temptations to seclusion; that early on the event you were with Sir Walter James in town, and passed the ensuing summer in travelling about with a friend.[214]

On the other hand, Bloom and Bloom state that a letter from Mrs Pennington to Mrs Piozzi at the time reported:

He [Thomas] is, as you may suppose, violently affected and strictly and earnestly prohibits all letters and visits of condolence which he says his mind cannot bear in its present and perturbed state... [215]

10.1 Elizabeth Whalley's memorial tablet in Burrington Church.

Thomas Sedgwick now withdrew to London, and while there learnt of the death of another good friend, the polymath Dr Erasmus Darwin.[216] This was followed by worries about the severe financial difficulties of his cousin, Sophia

Pennington, née Weston. Then, on 14th September, his venerable mother died in her 97th year. (Errors in the memorial plaque erected in Winscombe Church suggest that the funeral arrangements were left to his brother, Francis).

In January, 1802, Thomas was still staying in the house of his oldest friend, Sir Walter James, at 22 Devonshire Place, London. The Blagdon controversy was now at its height and Thomas was able to distract himself by working to assist Hannah More by composing the draft of his 'Animadversions', which would soon be added to the flurry of pamphlets which followed the reopening of her Blagdon school.[217]

It is suggested that his wife's death meant that Thomas Sedgwick was also distracted by an urgent need for money, as explained in Anna Seward's letter of that month:

> I grieve for Mr Whalley's irreparable loss, not only in a wife, so justly dear to him, but the means of obtaining a continuance of those expensive elegancies in his style of living, which long habit has rendered necessary to his comforts. I fear his wane of life will severely feel the inconvenience and deprivation resulting from the Quixotic generosity of his youth, when, as I have been informed, lest the world should think and say, and lest his beloved Mrs Sherwood should suspect, that his attachment was mercenary, he would not marry her till she had settled upon her own relations, after her death, all her maiden fortune except an annuity of £200. Her considerable jointure must drop with her.[218]

Yet by September, 1803, while Anna Seward is offering her condolences at the death of his mother, she was able to add:

> I am glad this second deprivation was withheld till you have found an object of affection equally dear with the two you have lost within the short space of a couple of years.[219]

This was Augusta Utica Heathcote, a wealthy spinster who he would marry on 19th May, 1803, at St. James Church, South Broom, Wiltshire, her family home. The witnesses were Augusta's brother Josiah, Eleanor Jones and Anna Cath Richards.

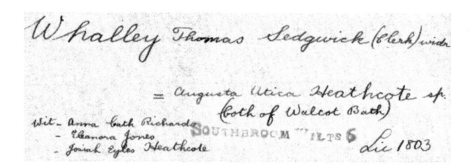

The marriage entry in the Southbroom church register.

The Heathcotes were an extensive, wealthy, influential and well-connected 18th and early 19th century family, with branches based in Derbyshire, Leicestershire and Wiltshire.

Augusta was the only surviving daughter of George Heathcote MP (1700-1768). Although born in Jamaica he had come to London in early life. He became a prosperous merchant and Member of Parliament, and was later elected Sheriff and Lord Mayor of London, but declined to serve in the latter office, pleading ill health, and thereupon retired to his country house near Devizes.[220]

Quite how Thomas Sedgwick and Augusta met is not known, but it seems likely this was through her brother, Josiah, as their father also owned a house in Walcot, Bath, and Josiah, who was born there in 1748, seems to have lived there until 1792. Josiah's memorial in St. Johns Church, Devizes, speaks of his courtesy, hospitality, polite manners and animated conversation, all of which are things which would have appealed to Thomas Sedgwick's circle of friends. According to Hill Wickham, after her marriage to Thomas in 1803, Augusta wrote to her friends of her great happiness and good fortune in being united to a gentleman `whom she had always admired beyond any of her acquaintances and who brought her a fortune equal to her own'.[221] It would seem, then, that she had known Thomas for some time before they were married and rather confirms that, after the death of her father in 1768, she either lived at Walcot or was a frequent visitor there.

As Augusta's father was said to be on very intimate terms with his cousins in Hursley,[222] it is quite possible that Thomas knew of her through the Rev Gilbert

Heathcote MA Oxon (1765- 1829). No less than 32 Heathcotes graduated from Oxford, and 16 held holy orders. As a former Vicar of Colerne, the Reverend Heathcote would have been well aware of Augusta's eligibility and wealth, as Colerne was only 16 miles from her home at South Broom House. (South Broom House is now a school). Gilbert was Archdeacon of Winchester and eventually became Treasurer of Wells in 1814, under the patronage of Bishop Richard Beadon, Thomas Sedgwick's cousin. In view of the timing of these events, Thomas Sedgwick may have used his influence on Bishop Beadon to assist his new wife's relative, Gilbert Heathcote, to become Treasurer. It also seems likely that the Heathcote influence was brought to bear as a quid pro quo when, in 1814, Robert Boyle Sullivan, who had been dismissed as curate of Winscombe in 1811 for dereliction of duties, found another curacy at Bradford-on-Avon, within the diocese of Salisbury, where he took over the stipendiary curacy from Thomas Heathcote (see Chapter 7).

The first indication that Thomas Sedgwick's proposal had been accepted was the Will which Augusta drew up on 18th May, 1803, the day before her marriage, but curiously this final Will was not signed until April three years later, and only six months before she died. Also, at the time of drawing up the Will, she gives the Royal Crescent as her address, but it may be that she was living there in the days before her marriage, as it would seem that, at this time, Thomas Sedgwick was back at Mendip Lodge, perhaps supervising rebuilding work.

Four days after their marriage, the couple were in Clifton, as Mendip Lodge was undergoing building work.[223] This may be indicative of the changes and expenses which the new Mrs Whalley brought to Thomas' life. A year later, perhaps as a result of this, Thomas sold Langford Court to the Rt. Hon John Hiley Addington, the brother of the Prime Minister, to whom it had been let in 1797.

There can be no doubt that the couple were exceedingly happy. Indeed, the new marriage seems rather to have gone to Thomas Sedgwick's head, incurring disapproval of some of his friends. The first intimations of this occurs in a letter from Anna Seward, dated 31st December, 1803:

I have heard much of the splendour of Mrs Whalley's jewels, of your plate, chandeliers and other magnificent ornaments for your board. However inconceivable to me that such exteriors can contribute to the happiness of a mind like yours, they must possess that power, or you would not have taken the trouble to purchase them and therefore I congratulate you on their possession.[224]

Six months later, her further comments are more in sorrow than in anger. Her letter of July 27th, 1804, starts out expressing sympathy over Thomas' recent poor health but soon focuses witheringly on its possible causes:

...it increases my wonder that its frequent and heavy pressure (of his continuing bad health) did not long since compel you to feel the comforts of leisure, rest, and the society of a few select friends, instead of condemning yourself in the decline of life, and loaded with pains and oppression, to the slavery of immense connections, which I understand was as little the taste of the present as of the late Mrs Whalley. Eternal crowds of company and superfluous magnificence, however they may excite exterior respect and selfish flattery, are sure to lessen instead of exalting him who invites the one and displays the other.

That I have heard many ridiculous exaggerations of Mr Whalley's imitation of the customs and manners of our dashing youthful nobility, I make no question; and when Admiral Brown's lady amused a circle of company at Buxton with accounts of the permitted public display of his bride's night clothes decorated with lace at the most profuse expense, I venture to say that she must have been misinformed for that Mr Whalley was a man of talents and however he might like to live splendidly could not have allowed a circumstance to exist so flagrantly open to just ridicule.

I mention these things with some hope of convincing you how much the reverse of respectability is all needless "prominence" as you term it from the station of life we were born and educated to fill. Increase of wealth and connection with those who are one step above us, can never make it our duty to follow the example of the light and vain in the higher ranks of society.

Flatterers will not speak this language ; a sincere friend will not repress it when its disclosure may possibly guard those beloved from future evils. [225]

Curiously, the earliest mention of the name Heathcote in Thomas Sedgwick's own correspondence occurs much later, in an undated letter addressed to Mendip Lodge in about the year 1805. This was an invitation from Hannah More to Thomas and a Mr Heathcote to share a meal of *'plain fare'* with her and William Wilberforce, who was with her at Barley Wood for a few days.[226] This seems very likely to have been Augusta's brother Josiah, who would by now have been living at South Broom House and doubtless had been invited to view the newly refurbished Mendip Lodge. There is, though, the possibility that this could have been Gilbert Heathcote, mentioned previously, who was still Vicar of Hursley parish, south west of Winchester, but who, in 1814, would become Treasurer of Wells Cathedral. Whoever it was, he was clearly staying with Thomas and his wife at Mendip Lodge.

The letter goes on to state that, at this short notice: *'I dare not venture to request the honour of seeing Mrs Whalley to dinner'*. This may have been Mrs More's way of suggesting that her presence would dampen the animated conversation. This would fit, as Anna Seward had described Augusta as *'gentle kind and good, and sensible though reserved'*.[227]

In April, 1806, Thomas Sedgwick found that extensive repairs were needed to the reservoir which supplied water to Mendip Lodge and its gardens. This rendered the house uninhabitable for the early summer, when he would normally reside there. He therefore took the opportunity to take his wife on a tour of England, as far north as York. Sadly, the second Mrs Whalley did not live long. According to Hill Wickham, Augusta caught a cold *'on leaving a crowded assembly in Bath'* in the autumn of 1807, and died a few weeks later on October 10th. (The date of 1805 given by Hill Wickham seems to have been an error.[228]) Her death does seem to have been a real blow to Thomas, and his memorial tablet statement that *'he forcibly feels her loss'* is in marked contrast to the more restrained comments to his first wife's death. This memorial also includes a verse which seems to reflect the poems which previously had been reserved for his much loved sister Elizabeth and his mother:

When Death unthought of, from his secret Stand

Struck my Augusta his relentless Hand

Markd her for Heav'n, but the envenom'd Dart,

Thro' her has pierc'd, incurably, my Heart

Incurably, is there no Saviour found

To draw the Point and Poison from the Wound

Yes: If submissive to the Will of God

Thro' Faith and Hope, I bless the chast'ning Rod:

With those I honoured most, and lov'd the best,

Not only here my mortal Part shall rest,

But rais'd Immortal we shall meet above

Where all is perfect Peace and perfect Love.

Augusta's Will made bequests of £3,000 to a goddaughter and £500 to a cousin. The rest of her estate went to Thomas Sedgwick.

Augusta Whalley's memorial tablet which joined the other two in Burrington church put there by Thomas Sedgwick Whalley.

After her death, Thomas went to live with his sister and brother-in-law, Mary and James Wickham, in Frome, from where he received a letter of condolence from Anna Seward, dated 19th October.[229] Later he went to Malvern Wells then on to see his oldest friend George Warrington at Wrexham, returning via Mrs Piozzi's house, Brynbella, at St Asaph.

In June, 1808, Thomas made his way to Scotland, partly as a holiday but also to receive a Doctorate from the University of Edinburgh, which he did on July 10th. According to Hill Wickham, he had enlisted Sir Walter Scott to proffer the petition, believing that a DD from Edinburgh would be seen as more meritorious than one from Cambridge.[230] This is borne out by the letter of support addressed to 'Mr Scott' which was enclosed, unsealed, in a letter sent to Thomas Sedgwick by Anna Seward dated May 12th, which he received before he left for Scotland. In this, she says that "*your wish* (i.e. Thomas') *must be mine*", but she does also suggest that, like Handel, Thomas should decline to accept a doctorate.[231] It is also clear, from what she quotes from an earlier letter, that Walter Scott was extremely reluctant to help such literary gentlemen to '*profit by degrees*'. Her letter the following month, in which she expresses her delight that this Scottish holiday has improved his health, also rebukes him roundly for accepting the doctorate, which she says served no purpose unless he is seeking to achieve further '*Church dignities*'.[232]

While on his way to Scotland, Thomas had stayed at Bowness with Robert Vans Agnew.[233] Perhaps in gratitude for this, or maybe inspired by his visit, he dedicated '*Kenneth and Fenella*', described by him as his '*trifling poem*', to Agnew. This legendary tale, as he remarks himself, is connected to the tragedy of Macbeth, and describes the murder of Kenneth II by Fenella who, according to legend, was the grandmother or great aunt of Macbeth. The poem seems to have been written at the end of 1808 and published in 1809.[234]

In the winter of 1809, Thomas Sedgwick bought or rented a house in Baker Street, close to where his friends, the Siddons, lived in Upper Baker Street and not far away from Sir Walter and Lady James, some more old friends. For the next four years he lived mainly there. According to Hill Wickham, he entertained sumptuously, was a collector of paintings and had a weakness for items of expensive jewellery.[235] These were purchased from Messrs Rundell and Bridge, the Royal Jewellers of Ludgate Hill, whose work now sells for millions. It is not clear where this information comes from, how reliable it is, or who these jewels were for, since they are not mentioned in his Will. Perhaps the answer lies in the suggestion made by Mrs Piozzi, in April, 1808:

As to my expressed hope of hearing that you had made a third choice (of wife), I was perfectly serious there, conscious as I am that the comfort of your future days depends upon an event of that sort. You dote upon Mendip Lodge, and to make that little Eden indeed an Eden to you, it is necessary that you should have a partner in its delights, and that you should have friends around you to partake them also, and to receive from one dear to you those attentions which neither the habits of your life, your health, nor spirits permit that you yourself should pay. There is a lady of whom, from your youthful days, you have thought most highly, the titled relict of a man of worth and honour; a lady suitable to you in every respect. Clarissa (Elizabeth Cornwallis, niece of the Marquis of Cornwallis, Bishop of Coventry and Lichfield 1781-1824) first suggested the idea to me; persuasion is in your accents (sic); and we think it probable you would not sue in vain. You cannot, I think, mistake the person I allude to. [236]

Perhaps the lady suggested by Mrs Piozzi did not meet with his approval, or perhaps she could see no advantage in marrying a 62-year-old in poor health, but such a pattern of providing gifts and then seeking something in return appears to be Thomas Sedgwick's usual means of getting his own way. This method had worked in getting Mrs Siddons to perform his play *'Edwy and Edilda'* at Drury Lane, but a later gift of *'the beauteous and magnificent sables'* in 1802, [237] failed to achieve its desired effect for another play. On this occasion, Mrs Siddons says *'I thank you for your kind offer of Rosilda but at present it is not in my power to get it up'*.[238] There is no record of Thomas Sedgwick having written such a play but it seems clear that this is what it was. It is obvious that he was still engaged in writing poems at this time, for his cousin Mrs Pennington (née Weston) thanks him for the *'beautiful and elegant poem'* he sent to her in the summer of 1809.[239]

THE THIRD
MRS WHALLEY

THE FIRST SUGGESTION that the 67-year-old Dr Whalley was intending to marry yet again came in a letter from Thomas to Mrs Piozzi, dated 16th June, 1812.[240] It is clear that Mrs Horneck was well known to them both and Thomas speaks of her talents and uncommon merits which he had come to know over a period of 30 years of correspondence and *'confidential friendship'*.

The widowed Mrs Fanny Horneck was the daughter of Nathaniel Gould, later Lt. Colonel, who had married Frances Mary Buckworth in 1752. He had two children from this first marriage, Fanny (born 1755) and Bulkeley (Buckley), born 19th January, 1753, in Westminster, who would later become mad. When his first wife died in 1759, Nathaniel Gould, then a Captain, immediately married Elizabeth Cochrane, the cousin of the diarist Boswell's mother. This is why we know something about him. Boswell had first met Nathaniel in 1762 and, during the following months, he often dined with the Goulds and enjoyed their company. Fanny, who according to Hill Wickham was known to be clever and well connected,[241] nevertheless married late in life. This was to Major Charles Horneck, of the 62nd Regiment of Foot, in 1790 when she was already 35-years-old. She was Horneck's second wife. His first marriage, to Sarah Keppel in May, 1773, did not last long. Within a year, Sarah had absconded with a fellow officer, John Scawen. Charles petitioned for divorce and the marriage was dissolved by Act of Parliament in 1776.[242] Charles' second marriage took place in Bath and this seems to have been about the time that Thomas Sedgwick got to know Mrs Horneck, as by this time the Whalleys were entertaining lavishly at their house in Royal Crescent. We do not know where the Hornecks were living at this time but, by 1813 when Thomas married her, Fanny was living at 16 Queen Square, Bath.

Captain Charles Horneck had been a colourful character in his younger days, when he was known as the 'Military Macaroni'. The name came about when young men of the nobility and gentry, returning from their Grand Tours, adopted continental fashions and enjoyed the Italian dish first made fashionable in England through the 'Macaroni Club'.[243] The Macaronies were the foplings, fribbles, or beaux of the day. They were the subject of mockery, and doubt was cast on their masculinity, sexual preferences and general conduct. Walpole refers to them as early as 1764; but their height was in the early 1770s.

Charles Horneck bought his commission as Ensign in the 3rd Footguards in 1768. Later, as a Captain, he was based at St James barracks, where the guards had a reputation for parading in the nearby park in their finery and enjoying the attractions of London.[244]

This plate faces the first page of *The Macaroni and Theatrical Magazine* of October 1772.

General Horneck died on 8th April, 1804. In his Will of 8th August, 1802, he left his entire estate to '*Henry Genean my faithful servant*'. Mrs Horneck, who was still living in Bath at this time, was now free to remarry and, after seven years of widowhood, was approached by Dr Whalley. According to Hill Wickham, his friends had been urging him to remarry for some time, having '*no lady to preside at his table*'.[245] Thomas Sedgwick was now in his late sixties, Mrs Horneck 10 years his junior.

In a letter to Hester Piozzi dated 16th June, 1812, seven months before his third marriage, he wrote:

Mrs Lutwyche informed you of my fair prospect for the renewal of those domestic Comforts which I have, since I could observe, and reflect, valued above all others and without which the Life, of Life, with me, is gone- Your Lynx Eye, and quick perception, would enable you to distinguish Mrs Horneck's Talents and turn of mind, on a cursory acquaintance; but they could not give you the full knowledge of her various and uncommon merits, that I have after a confidential friendship and Correspondence with her of more than 30 years, -I know she likes you, and I think I know you well enough to be confident that you like her; and when you know each other au fond, which I trust you will do, you will esteem and have sincere affection for each other. [246]

Her reply, two weeks later, was as follows:

Brynbella Monday 29th June 1812

I direct to my Dear Doctor Whalley at Bath tho 'I do believe this anxious evening sees him at London at the Theatre (this was at the farewell performance of Sarah Siddons at the Garrick). *You who never forget old friends will feel for our charming Siddons, tho' your heart is once more taking irrevocable Engagements may they be happy as I wish, and as you deserve. It is impossible to know Mrs Horneck and not to love her, equally impossible not to see that she loves you; I am glad that things are to end so, and pray divide my cordial congratulations between you...* [247]

Given all this, it is difficult to entirely believe the account by De Quincey, though there is some truth in it:

Finding himself in difficulties by the expenses of this villa (Mendip Lodge) going on concurrently with another large establishment, he (TSW) looked out for a good third marriage as the sole means within his reach of clearing off his embarrassments without proportionable curtailment of his expenses. It happened, unhappily for both parties, that he fell in with a widow lady who was cruising about the world with precisely the same views and in precisely the same difficulties. Each (or the friends of each) held out a false flag, magnifying their incomes respectively, and sinking the embarrassments. Mutually deceived they married, and one change immediately introduced at the splendid villa was the occupation of an entire wing by a lunatic brother of the lady's, the care of whom with a large allowance had been made to her by the Court of Chancery. This, of itself, shed a gloom over the place, which defeated the primary purpose of the Doctor (as explained by himself) in erecting it. Windows barred, maniacal howls, gloomy attendants from a lunatic hospital ranging about—these were the sad disturbances to the Doctor's rose-leaf system of life.[248]

This lithograph of a painting by Maxim Gauci is the only known portrait of Mrs Horneck Whalley.
It probably dates from 1813-1814 after which point the couple separated. © National Portrait Gallery, London.

The couple married on 5th October, 1813, and initially lived at 16 Queen Square, Bath. This had at one time been General Horneck's address, though whether he rented or owned the property is not clear. This was a sensible arrangement as Thomas Sedgwick had sold his house in Royal Crescent after the death of his second wife, and it was now the beginning of the Bath season. The following month Mrs Siddons, now retired from the Garrick Theatre, read Macbeth to them both at this address.[249] According to Hill Wickham, his great uncle soon discovered that his third wife had debts of many thousands of pounds, which he now was obliged to pay off.[250] By July of the following year the couple had moved to Thomas Sedgwick's usual summer residence of Mendip Lodge,[251] this time accompanied by her mad brother (Bulkeley Gould, 1753-1727) who the Court of Chancery had placed in the care of Mrs Horneck. This was too much for Thomas, for whom Mendip Lodge had always been his source of solace and joy. In a letter to Mrs Piozzi, dated 2nd July, he writes:

This once darling place is become a gilded millstone for me. As it would be a Folly and a Sin to keep at great Expense, what I can no longer hope to enjoy, I am looking out sharply, on all sides for a purchaser, of a Place and Property, highly attractive and eligible for a Person who has good Health fine Taste and a large Fortune. All the furniture is to be sold with the house etc....The Malady of my Chest, and, as wise Doctors say, of the bottom of my Wind pipe increases so much and made such a miserable Creature of me the whole of last Winter and Spring, that I have determined to....seek a milder and more settled climate somewhere in France......Mrs Whalley cannot leave the Charge of her poor brother; nor indeed would she like the Journey and Voyage, or the accommodation and mode of living on the Continent. Her habits of Life and turn of Mind are peculiar, and new ones even with bonne Volonté, are not easily adopted, at 58 – Your old and true Friend, therefore is to become a wanderer at 68.... [252,253]

Two days later, Mrs Piozzi replies:

Ah my Dear kind Friend my ever faithfully attached Doctor Whalley! And must we really part so without an well founded hope of meeting again in this

World? Your sweet Letter would have taken my Breath quite away had not our beloved (Mrs) Siddons prepared me for its reception. Neither She nor I however can say a Word against your very rational Plan: Health is the first Thing to be considered, and as You say- our Lives are of Consequence to our Successors. I am glad I saw Mendip (Lodge) in its full Beauty and Glory – very glad. I have now seen the most beautiful place in England; under Possession of a Friend I must forever love and respect.[254]

To all but his closest friends, the reason for Dr Whalley's retreat to France was on the grounds of his health but it is clear that the couple did not really get on. So he left for the continent alone; alone, that is, apart from his personal assistant Walter Amans, his servant John, his coachman and its two postillions!

By October 10th, he was in Orleans and planning to move south to Nevers shortly. Writing to his lifelong friend Arthur Anstey, he asks him to direct any person who might be interested in purchasing Mendip Lodge to his bailiff, Mr Naish.[255]

Thomas remained in Nevers over the winter of 1814/5. It is clear from Hannah More's letter to him, in February, that his apartments there were spacious and that his niece, Mrs Boyle Sullivan, was with him.[256] Here he enjoyed the company and hospitality of his old friend Count Coëtlosquet, now the general of the district and a lively cultured man. The Count's military connections meant that he had early knowledge of Napoleon's escape from Elba at the end of February, 1815, at the start of his 'one hundred days'. The Count wrote immediately of urging Thomas Sedgwick to flee ('*Partez de suite et le plus tôt possible sera lent à retourner en Angleterre, sans vous arrêter*').[257] He did not follow this advice but, confident in the abilities of the Duke of Wellington, retreated first to Mons, at the time an important allied base, and then to Leuven, 20 miles to the east of Brussels, which was within a few hours by fast coach from Antwerp, should he need to make a hasty escape!

Immediately after the Battle of Waterloo, Thomas wrote to his sister, Mrs Wickham, giving a vivid account of his observations and experiences, a section of which is reproduced here. The whole, with the observations of his great nephew, indicates how fully informed Thomas was. It should be remembered that, by this time, he was only accompanied by his servant John Clark,[258] his

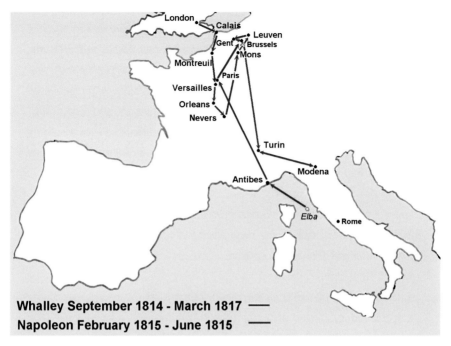

Whalley's travels 1814-1817 and Napoleon's 100 days.

friend Amans having returned to England.

> *Though distant above thirty miles from the field (of battle),I distinctly heard the roar of artillery for twelve hours, and could perceive that it advanced and became louder on the left, where the Prussians were so far defeated as to fall considerably back. Night luckily came to their assistance, added to the extreme exhaustion of the French to whom some hours' repose became absolutely necessary...*

> *There was no affair on the 17th except between Blucher's rearguard and some French cavalry and light troops, Meanwhile, the Duke had reinforced his army with two of our best regiments of infantry cantoned between Brussels and Termond (sic) with nearly ten thousand of our matchless cavalry...*

> *The field of battle being not more than five little leagues from Louvain, the thunder of artillery and musketry shook the windows at which I stood. From*

three to five the momentary roar of war grew louder; from five to seven it neither increased nor decreased ; from seven till half past nine it became, to my great joy fainter and fainter. But while I was reassuring the loyal and worthy family in whose house I lodged that the French were evidently beaten and retiring, various persons, some of them very intelligent and respectable, came in with haggard looks and confidently asserted that the Prussian Army was entirely routed, and that Lord Wellington was slowly retiring though disputing every inch of ground to Brussels...

...I now began to think that my ear had greatly deceived me; and, as I could fly but not fight I had been foolhardy in placing such implicit confidence in the Duke of Wellington for my protection...

As necessity had no law, I threw myself humbly on the protection of the Almighty, and submitted with trembling to my fate. Fatigued, agitated and harassed, I was preparing to go to bed, when the post-horse master and another gentleman, kindly came to assure me that I might sleep and stay here in peace, as certain news had arrived that the great French army were (sic) defeated at all points and retreating in the greatest disorder...[259]

After three months at Leuven, Thomas travelled to Gand (Ghent) and then to Brussels in November, where he stayed a further three months with William Mullins, his wife and their 18-year-old heir, who William had so earnestly desired, but whose second wife, Thomas Sedgwick's niece Frances, had failed to produce. Thomas has nothing but praise for his *'old and steady friend'* and his family for their courtesy and charms.[260]

By April, 1815, Mrs Horneck Whalley, for so she seemed now to be known,[261] had left Mendip Lodge, which was now in the sole care of Thomas Sedgwick's bailiff. According to Mrs Piozzi, Mrs Horneck Whalley was living in a cottage *'within sight of the Mendip Lodge'*, forced to do so on financial grounds.[262] Despite being on the continent, the sale of Mendip Lodge was still very much on Thomas' mind. According to Hill Wickham, in December, 1815, he wrote the following from Brussels to his legal adviser Arthur Anstey, son of Christopher Anstey:

Next summer a favourable offer may be made for Mendip Lodge, or, if not next year the following one. However straitened my income, I will contrive to live under it. I have been guilty of too much waste, and too many follies in money matters; but those who come after me, shall not have to reproach my memory for sacrificing their interest to the selfishness of selling, at a very inferior value, such a property as will one day not only sell for, but be well worth, the sum I now demand for it viz £30,000. [263]

By the end of March, 1818, Whalley was back in Bath and had purchased the central house (No 5) at Portland Place.[264] This he furnished lavishly and elegantly and when Mrs Piozzi viewed it, on June 6th, she said she had seldom seen such splendid apartments.[265] Thomas Sedgwick's first recorded letter from his new address is to his great nephew, and is dated July, 1818. Hill Wickham was now aged 11 years, and had just visited there. Thomas expresses the hope that his great nephew will be able to visit again during the Christmas holidays.[266] Hill Wickham would write later that the house in Portland Place had been bought by this great uncle with every intention of his remaining there for the rest of his life. Sadly, this was soon to change. [267]

In July, 1819, Thomas finally sold Mendip Lodge to Benjamin Somers as he had always hoped to do. Only three months later, Thomas' wife deserted him under a plea of ill treatment.[268] A letter from Mrs Piozzi to the actor Conway, dated 1st September, 1819, reported: '*old Whalley's wife running away from him and settling in Freshford*'.[269] But in a slightly earlier letter, to John Salusbury, she recounts that Mrs Whalley Horneck had long been wishing to part from her new husband and had now taken her mad brother and herself off while Thomas was away.[270] This event was soon well known in Bath and was reported by Mrs Piozzi in a letter dated 29th October, 1819, to their mutual friend Mrs Pennington:

Dr and Mrs Whalley seem to have been giving la comedie gratis here while the theatres are shut up. Incidents are certainly not wanting and the Catastrophe kept quite out of site as Bayes recommends, for purpose of elevating and surprising. Those who come to hear what I say on the subject go home disappointed for I say nothing and indeed have nothing to say. [271]

Various conjectures circulated as to Mrs Horneck Whalley's reason for "running off" but according to Hill Wickham it was her accusation of cruelty which forced Thomas Sedgwick to seek a legal separation.[272] Mrs Whalley subsequently attempted to correspond with him but Hill Wickham says he *'never again addressed her'*. While the grounds for separation were incompatibility, it would seem that Thomas also made efforts to prove that his wife was now as mad as her brother Bulkeley and her mother had been before him. Her brother owned estates in Bovington near Berkhamstead and in June 1826 Mrs Horneck appealed to the Court of Chancery for control of these doubtless to fund her own lifestyle!

After they separated their friends were divided in their allegiances. Most sided with Thomas but the influential Mrs Lutwyche and a few others sided with Mrs Whalley and this group seem to have had no further contact with Thomas Sedgwick.[273] As part of a *'comfortable settlement'* which Thomas was required to provide his wife as part of the legal separation, Mrs Horneck Whalley gained a large house at 2 Catherine Place, just north of Royal Crescent.[274] According to Hill Wickham Mrs Whalley was thereafter known in Bath for her *'handsome parties'*.[275] The house was well suited to these having 16 rooms and having been owned by the wealthy Miss Wroughton, the one time Queen of Bath.

One of Mrs Hornecks famous parties was held in September 1824 this time at her *'mansion'* in Queen Square. This might suggest that she had sold 2 Catherine Place in order to return to her old address in fashionable Queen Square where she had lived before her marriage to Whalley. However an advertisement shortly before her death in the Belvedere on 16th September 1832 announced that an auction was to be held of her effects at 2 Catherine Place which she must have somehow retained until that time.[276, 277]

On Tuesday Mrs. Whalley gave a Private Concert at her mansion in Queen Square, consisting of ah admirable selection of vocal and instrumental music from the works of Handel, Haydn, Mozart, Rossini, &c. The Concert was under the direction of Mr. C. W. Manners, who displayed great taste in the arrangements. In the course of the evening a beautiful original concerted piece, written by Mrs. Whalley, and composed by Mr. Manners, was twice performed: it is very effective, and was received with enthusiastic delight: the subject of the piece is an elegant tribute of friendship to the Duc D'Angouleme.

From the Bath Journal of 14 September 1824.

CHAPTER 10

THE FINAL YEARS

ALMOST IMMEDIATELY AFTER Mrs Horneck Whalley '*ran off*' to Freshford in the late summer of 1819, Thomas abandoned public life in Bath, where he was now the subject of ridicule, and viewed his '*gala days*' as now being over.[278] He let the house he had only recently purchased in Portland Place and he went to lodge with his sister and brother-in-law in Frome.[279]

In July of that year, he had been confident that Mendip Lodge, which had become a burden to him, had been sold to Benjamin Somers '*to his great content*'.[280] The contentment was because he had always felt unhappy about the breaking of the entail which was started by his first wife's first husband, John Sherwood, and which had denied the Somers family ownership of Langford Court after her death.

Despite the footnote in Hill Wickham's book, which says the sale was never completed,[281] there is no doubt whatsoever that the sale took place and the house and estate were purchased by Benjamin Somers on 14th June, 1819, for £22,500, though subject to a mortgage of £15,000, to Arthur Anstey Calvert, Thomas Sedgwick's legal adviser.[282, 283]

Free from both his third wife and the burden of Mendip Lodge, Thomas Sedgwick set sail for France in April, 1820, to visit his dear niece Frances Sullivan (née Sage). After a rough crossing from Brighton to Dieppe, he made his way to La Flèche via Rouen, Bernay, Alençon and Le Mans, accompanied by his ever faithful manservant John. On May 29th, 1820, he was able to write to his great nephew:

La Flèche is rather a pretty town in a pleasant and fertile country. There is a famous extensive and handsome college here (This was the famous National Military Academy)*, where languages, mathematics, military sciences etc are*

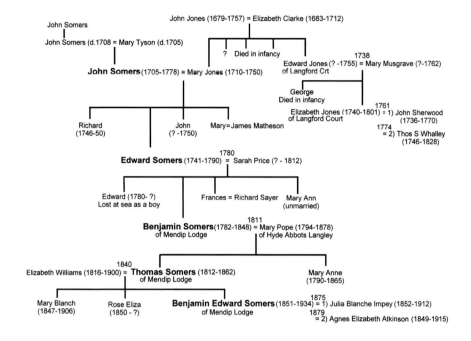

The Somers family and its relationship to Elizabeth Whalley née Jones.

taught under the best preceptors, and which is governed by a general and a colonel. The latter (besides several other gentlemen) has visited me, and is a noble looking, well bred and agreeable man. Mrs Sullivan, my niece and your cousin was overjoyed to see me. The house she has engaged for me is one of the best in the town. I have a handsome drawing room, a large saloon opening into it, a dining parlour on the other side of a vestibule, a large kitchen, and other offices and a large and beautiful bed chamber, with a dressing room for myself and a good bedchamber for John (his manservant) and an inferior one for a French servant. My best apartments look in to a pretty flower garden full now with various sorts of roses in full bloom, and the house standing within a court, is shut up at night. I am as quiet here as if I was twenty miles from a town. I shall have a very select and agreeable society who will come to me four or five times a week, to chat or play whist and a game called Boston.[284]

It will be recalled that Frances and her second husband, the Reverend Robert

Boyle Sullivan, had moved there from England sometime after the signing of the second Treaty of Paris, in November, 1815, but this was Thomas' first visit to the town. It is clear from his letter that the Sullivans lived comfortably in France but there is no clue as to how their life was financed or whether the Reverend Robert Boyle Sullivan was employed as an Anglican priest while living there. In fact, there is no mention whatsoever of Robert Sullivan on any page of the two volumes edited by Hill Wickham.[285] During that summer of 1820, Thomas became very well established in La Flèche and a respected member of the local community. This is not surprising; he already spoke fluent French (though we are told with a terrible accent), and was a royalist who was well connected with French society from his earlier visits to the continent.

About this time, rumours began to circulate in England that Mendip Lodge was to be bought by the Duchess of York. There must have been some hope that this would happen, as the main bedroom at the rear of the house had, by this time, become known as the "Duchess of York's bedroom". A press report in the 1950s describes the Lodge as being *'almost bought by Queen Caroline'.*[286] This seems to be a repeat of the claim by Coyshe et al.

The state bedroom, like the dining-room, is at the back, and was fitted up with much magnificence in expectation of its being occupied by the late Duchess of York on an intended visit to this spot.[287]

This would have been Caroline of Brunswick, who had separated from her husband, the Duke of York, later George IV, almost immediately after their marriage and, since 1814, had been living rather scandalously on the continent. Whatever the truth of her interest in Mendip Lodge, a public denial by the owner Benjamin Somers appeared first in the Bristol Gazette in 1821 and was then reprinted in the Morning Post of July 16th.[288]

Quite when Thomas returned to England is not clear. Hill Wickham is rather confused about this period, which is not surprising when he himself was away at school.[289] As a consequence, there are few letters included by him at this time. He states that *'with the exception of the winter of 1823, which he (TSW) spent with his niece Mrs Sullivan, he visited among his relatives until 1825',* [290] but sometime early in 1822, Thomas had returned to England. This is

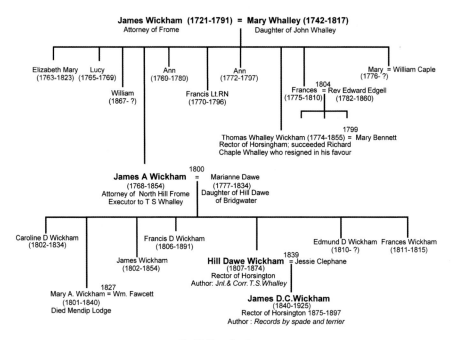

The Wickham family tree.

likely to have been because of the concerns of his solicitor and executor James Anthony Wickham, or perhaps a letter from Benjamin Somers himself, who had found he was unable to keep up the mortgage payments on Mendip Lodge. As a result, on 10th May, 1822, Thomas bought the house, its original contents, and the estate, back for £5,000 less that he had sold it for.

One might have expected Somers to have now moved out and Thomas Sedgwick to have reoccupied the house but this does not seem to have happened. It is quite possible that he allowed Somers to continue living there as a tenant, which would account for him still being identified as the owner in December, 1822.

Thomas then spent a comfortable winter of 1822/3 with his cousin by marriage, formerly Penelope Weston now Mrs Pennington, and her husband, in Dowry Square, Bristol, arriving there in November, 1822.[291] Penelope's original invitation had extended to Mrs Sullivan but it is not clear if the latter joined them there. By August, 1823, Thomas was back in France, this time staying at Versailles with Frances for the summer. Their address was the finest: the Avenue de Sceaux, one of three roads that radiated from the Place d'Armes in front of the Palace of Versailles. Once again, there is no mention of Frances' husband, Robert Boyle Sullivan, who was to die only a year later.

Thomas wrote from Versailles to his great nephew, who was now home at Frome from Lord Weymouth's Grammar School, Warminster:

The summer is drawing to its close with less sunshine (except in 1816) than I ever remember. Within doors I have all the comforts that spacious, commodious, pleasant and warm apartments can bestow, added to the affectionate attentions and animated and entertaining conversation of my dear niece Mrs Sullivan who never leaves me except to go out about housekeeping concerns, or to call on our few acquaintances. One agreeable and very respectable family from Shropshire named Owen I have lately discovered to be temporary inhabitants of this noble town. The mother of Mrs Owen, Mrs Cummins, was one of my oldest friends...

...My weak health has prevented me from going to Paris to visit several noble families, and particularly Count Coetlosquet who is, and who merits to be, high in the King's favour and is director general with the war with Spain. He is reckoned to be one of the cleverest, and is certainly one of the best-bred and most agreeable men in France. But as I cannot go to him, overwhelmed as he is with the most important affairs,he has very kindly promised to come and dine with me and Mrs Sullivan at Versailles next Sunday se'nnight....[292]

Thomas returned to England in October, 1823, as he had always intended.

Perhaps remembering his pleasant stay with the Penningtons in Dowry Square two years before, he now purchased the lease of 4, Windsor Terrace, Clifton, at its spectacular location above the Avon Gorge. This was only a few hundred yards from his cousin Penelope Pennington's house in Dowry Square, and close to the house in Clifton where his lifelong friend Mrs Piozzi frequently stayed. Windsor Terrace had been completed in 1820 by William Watts. He had made a fortune from discovering how to make perfectly round lead shot, then almost bankrupted himself in building the terrace. Thomas' first letter from his new house is dated November, 1825.

Thomas' house in Windsor Terrace Clifton (arrowed) viewed from the Cumberland Basin Swing Bridge over the River Avon.

Windsor Terrace, given to Hannah More in 1826. Sadly the plaque only records Hannah's occupation and not that of its original owner the Rev Dr Thomas Sedgwick Whalley who had made it over to her.

Sadly, a letter which Thomas received at Frome from his old friend, the Marquise de la Pierre, dated March 28th, 1826, reveals that only a few months after he had leased it, Thomas' new Clifton house in Windsor Terrace had not suited him and he was now recovering from yet another illness.[293] However, Hill Wickham says that his great uncle had only imagined that the fogs of the Avon were the cause of his latest health problem.[294]

Hannah More and Windsor Terrace

Little has been said until now about another of Thomas' close friends: Hannah More, the playwright and educationalist, about whose life much has been written.[295, 296, 297] It is not clear how well Thomas Sedgwick Whalley knew her before his involvement in resolving the Blagdon Controversy, which greatly affected Miss More during 1800-2, but thereafter they were very close friends. In 1801, Hannah and her sisters moved from their cottage in Cowslip Green, where the first Mrs Whalley had been taken after her coach accident in April, 1789, to a house they had built for themselves near Wrington, called Barley Wood. From here, Hannah could look across the valley to the whitewashed Mendip Lodge, which she called "*Mont Blanc*". She and her sisters lived happily there for many years and received many visitors, but by 1819, Hannah was alone. For some years she suffered poor health and was rarely out of her bedroom but then, in 1826, she discovered her servants had been cheating her out of substantial sums.

The following account is taken from Henry Thompson's book of 1838:[295]

Mrs More resolved, in bitterness of heart, to sever from the cherished abode of seven and-twenty years, and remove to Clifton. The Rev Dr Whalley, ever Miss. More's steady and generous friend, allowed her to take immediate possession of his house at Clifton, (One assumes that because of his financial position Thomas made over the lease to the wealthy Hannah More) *and J. S, Harford, Esq., of Blaise Castle would send his carriage to convey her. Miss More's advisers had determined to remove her to Clifton as soon as practicable, giving the servants no notice of the day, but paying them, on the morning, a quarters wages in advance. The plan was ripe for execution on the 18th of April.*

When the hour was come when she was to step into the carriage which waited to convey her to Clifton, she descended the stairs and contemplated in silence, for a few minutes, the portraits of beloved friends which covered the walls of her dining room and left never to return.

The house at Clifton, (No. 4, Windsor Terrace,) which had been selected for her abode, commanded, from behind, a bold and varied prospect. The scene, no sooner met the eye of Hannah More, than it awakened a beautiful and pious reflection, "I was always," she said, "delighted with fine scenery; but my sight, of late years, has been too dim to discern the distant beauties of the Vale of Wrington. It has pleased Providence to ordain me, in my last days, a view no less beautiful, all the features of which my eye can embrace."

In this state of calm acquiescence in the lot appointed her, her elastick mind soon recovered from its depression, and she was again able to enjoy conversation with the social and intelligent. Her conversation had lost nothing of its brilliancy;

This is borne out by the report, by the same author, that she received 400 visitors in the first three weeks of her residence.

The final farewells

By now, Thomas Sedgwick, aged 80, realised he did not have very long to live, and set about trying to put his affairs in order. In January, 1826, he wrote, resigning his position as Prebend of Wells.[298] He was still making efforts to sell Mendip Lodge and set about making the property more attractive and accessible by adding a new drive through the park, with two entrance lodges, where it joined the West Harptree Turnpike. Much to his delight, he was able to drive up it for the first time, *"furred like a Russian"*, in March, 1827. While the lodges were destroyed by fire in the 1960s the drive remains and is still used by a local shooting syndicate.

The Pepperpot Lodges added in 1826.

Thomas was also trying to retrieve the interest, if not the capital sum of £500, owing to him from William Mullins, who had been Frances Sullivan's first husband. William had, in 1824, become the second Lord Ventry and inherited the long-awaited fortune from his very long-lived father from which, under their agreement, the loan was now due to be repaid. Thomas' letter, dated April 27th, 1827, to his solicitor Mr Bromley, complained about Mullins' continuing failure to settle the debt, and is uniquely vitriolic.[299] It is possible that the Whalley estate never recovered this sum, although there were clear instructions in Thomas Sedgwick's Will that this was still owing and James Wickham, Thomas' executor, would certainly have pursued this claim.

During the winter of 1827/8, Thomas Sedgwick had again been far from well. In December, he was living with his elder brother at Winscombe Court, from where he wrote to his nephew, Hill Wickham, who was about to take his final degree examinations at Oxford, saying that he expected to spend Christmas in bed.[300] However, by April the following year, he was sufficiently well to return to Clifton where, he says in a further letter to his nephew, he bid a last sad farewell to Hannah More at Windsor Terrace:

Yesterday I went to bid a last sad adieu to my dear admirable old friend Mrs H.

More. I sat two hours with her, and, ye gods! we talked – how we did talk! [301]

By this time, Thomas had learnt of the financial predicament of his dearly loved niece, Frances Sullivan, now two years a widow but still living in La Flèche. In 1818, her father had died believing her to be well provided for under the terms of her divorce settlement and so, apart from a *"ring as a token of my remembrance"*, she received nothing from him. While Frances' annuity should have continued for the rest of her life, with the death of the first Lord Ventry, and the confusion over settling his estate, this ceased; she was now penniless. Thomas determined to go to France to rescue her from her financial difficulties. On 14th July, 1828, the same day as he amended his Will, he wrote to his great nephew, Hill Wickham, from London to explain his decision:

My choice therefore lay, especially after knowing of Mrs Sullivan's distress, between La Flèche and Exeter* and all the circumstances impartially considered, none of my English friends can wonder at my preferment of the former to the latter, for my residence next autumn, winter and spring. Beyond the latter I dare not extend my views though should I be so fortunate as to sell beautiful Mendip Lodge this year and my life be prolonged by wintering in a warmer climate I would do the utmost to engage Mrs Sullivan to accompany me back to England and live in some snug and pleasant house. [302]

*because of its milder winter climate

He told his nephew he was now in rather better health and so would make the journey by several stages in his carriage, taking four or six stops per day and so no one should have any fear for him. He anticipated arriving in La Flèche on or shortly after 28th July, but the exact date is not known. On arrival, he dictated Codicil to his Will in French and subsequently this was translated as follows, and then added to his 16-page English Will:

I Thomas Sedgwick Whalley DD do hereby acknowledge to you the Executor of my last Will and Testament that I owe my niece Mrs Frances Elizabeth Sullivan otherwise Sage widow of the late Revd. Boyle Sullivan residing at La Flèche

Frances' new house at 6 Rue Vernevelle La Flèche as it is today.

Department of the Sarthe In France the sum of one thousand and fifty two pounds sterling which she lent to me and which I am bound to repay her as follows Viz four hundred and fifty two pounds sterling on the twenty fifth day of December one thousand eight hundred and twenty eight and six hundred pounds sterling on the twenty fifth day of June one thousand eight hundred and twenty nine I order you the Executor of my last Will and testament in case my death should take place before the payment of the abovementioned Debt to pay my niece Mrs Frances Elizabeth Sullivan the aforesaid sum of One thousand and fifty two pounds sterling out of my property before any Legacy or other sum of money whatsoever in Devonshire.[303]

He then made arrangements to buy the house at 6 rue Vernevelle La Flèche for Frances. This still is one of the most magnificent houses in the town. Built in the early 18th century for Louis Huger de la Molière, it is now a listed National Monument. It currently houses a centre for the contemporary arts and is known as Hôtel Huger.

Why did he buy this large house for a 59-year-old English widow? Perhaps this was felt by both of them that it was a wise investment and owning such

Dr Thomas Sedgwick's tomb in the cemetery of St Thomas, La Flèche.

a house would mean Frances was no longer liable for any rent she might have otherwise had to pay out of her reduced income. Maybe he had intended to live there with her. The purchase was transacted by a mortgage with a deposit of 6,000F, with other payments due on 25th June, 1829, and a final payment to be made no later than 21st November, 1829.

Thomas had made a great impression on La Flèche society when he stayed there during his previous extended visits from the summer of 1820 until late in 1822, during which time he regularly played cards with the senior officers of the Military Academy. Thus when Thomas died peacefully in his armchair in Mrs Sullivan's house at Faubourg Saint-Jacques on 4th September, 1828,[304] the wishes of visiting Anglicans were over-ruled by the local residents and Thomas was buried at La Flèche in the burial ground of the Roman Catholic church of St. Thomas. His final resting place was initially railed off but these railings have since been lost. The tomb, however, is still there. An Anglican clergyman came out from Nantes to officiate at the funeral.[305] The fact that the Staffords and the Sullivans were living only 30 miles apart in France explains why General Stafford, doubtless accompanied by his wife, Frances' cousin, was able to attend the funeral. The only other attendee mentioned by Hill Wickham was Mr Torriano, the son of one of his oldest friends, Major Torriano.

The inscription is as shown opposite, which is curiously not quite the same as that set out in Hill Wickham's book, from which one must conclude that he never visited the grave of his great uncle. It looks rather as if what had been written in England by Thomas' executor was modified on site by the person who supervised the engraving.

THOMAE SEDGWICK WHALLEY SANCTAE THEOLOGIIAE DOCTORIS
EX COMITATU SOMERSETTIAE, CUI MAGISTRATUS PRAERAT
IN ANGLIA
ECCLESIAE CATHEDRALIS WELLENSIAE PRAEBENDARII
VIGEBANT IN EO BENEVOLENTIA ERGA DEUM PIETAS
BENEVOLENTIA ERGA HOMINES VERE CHRISTIANA
LIBERALITAS ERGA EGENOS EFFUSA
HUMANITATEM VILLAE FORMOSISSIMAE SUAE MENDIP VICINIAE
TESTANTUR
AMORE ITAQUE QUEM PER LONGAM VITAM
INGENII EXCELLENTIA ET MOREM SUAVITATE
CONCILIARAT
MORTE TANDEM IN DESIDERIUM ACERRIMUM COMMUTATO
ONIMBUS CHARUS SUIS CHARISSIMUS
OBIT TERIO DIE SEP. A.D.. MDCCCXXVIII
AETATIS SUAE LXXXIII

It should perhaps be added that De Quincey's widely-quoted contention that Whalley died '*in a common lodging house... in all things the very antithesis of that splendid abode which he had planned for the consolation of his melancholy and the gay beguilement of his old age*' has not the slightest foundation in truth.[306] Whether De Quincey was misled or added this out of pure spite can only be guessed at, but it is clear from this, and earlier accounts, that De Quincey, who as a boy had lived close to the Whalleys in Bath, disliked Thomas Sedgwick and his lifestyle intensely.

The news of Thomas' death was in the English newspapers within two weeks.[307] It is possible that Frances herself would have undertaken to take the news and the Codicil to Thomas' Will to England, or it could have been his faithful servant John Clark who, in any case, would have had to return to England taking Thomas' personal effects and his carriage. Under the terms of the Will, Thomas' executor James Wickham took over the ownership of Mendip Lodge, and John Clarke received one year's full wages of fifty guineas plus a further sum of £220. By the following year, Rutter, in his book, was describing Mendip Lodge as *'The seat of the late Dr Whalley and property of James Anthony Wickham of North Hill Frome'*. [308]

Postscript - *What happened to Frances Sullivan?*

A popular belief is that Frances lived on quietly in France in poverty, sadly recalling her days as *'Queen of Bath'*, but this is quite untrue.[309] One would assume, from the purchase of the house at 6 Rue Vervenelle, which Thomas had paid for, that Frances had intended to continue to live on in France, yet two years later, on 3rd September, 1830, she sold the house to Edouard Le Monnier de Lorrière and his wife for 26,000F. This change of mind was probably precipitated by the unrest in France which preceded the end of the Bourbon dynasty. There had been three poor harvests between 1826-1829 and food was now in short supply in France. Perhaps the final spur for Frances' departure was the riot of March 24, 1830, in Merdrignac, only 100 miles from La Flèche.[310] By 26th July, there was full revolution against the Bourbons in Paris, followed by the abdication of Charles X on 2nd August.[311]

Where Frances then went is unknown but she probably went directly to Bath. While its hey-day was past it was still a fashionable place to be but, rather than being the haunt of East Indiamen seeking eligible young brides, it was now becoming the home of retired elderly gentry. Sir Isaac Pitman, the inventor of shorthand, who would later retire to Royal Crescent, put it: *'Of the many beautiful cities in this fair country, Bath is unquestionably the most beautiful'*.[312]

What is known is that Frances was in Bath by 1841, as the census of that year records her as living in Gloucester Place with her 30-year-old servant Nancy Price. This was a district consisting largely of lodging houses, and Frances' address was run by a female lodging house keeper, Mary Roberts, with four other female inhabitants and one male occupant. Gloucester Place was severely damaged in the Bath Baedeker raids of World War II and no longer exists, but had been described in Egan's Guide of 1819 as being of no particular architectural merit.[313]

There was much to occupy a widow in Bath by this time, all of which would have been accessible by Sedan chair. The new Theatre Royal remained open until 1862. The Pump Room Orchestra continued to operate and, in 1843, the Bath Literary and Scientific Institution admitted lady members. Here, papers were presented on a wide variety of topics and such was the level of interest in Bath that the 34th meeting of the British Association for the Advancement of Science was held there in 1864. All this would have kept the well-educated Frances Sullivan amused.

By 1851, Frances was able to move to more desirable rooms at 2 Paragon Buildings. Perhaps the move followed the final settling of Thomas Sedgwick's estate. The census of that year describes three households as occupying the house: Thomas Peggs was the lodging keeper, with his wife, daughter and niece; two other occupants were described as dressmakers and there was also a physician, Dr Morewood, aged 70 years. Frances is described as a 75-year-old *"annuitant"* living with her 40-year-old servant Sarah Mercer from Chew Stoke, though Frances was now 81-years-old!

Her annuity must have come came partly from the sale of her house in France, which raised 26,000F in 1830 (about £1,000 Sterling), but the 5% UK interest rate at the time would only have provided Frances with an income of £50 p.a. so she must have had other sources. These could have been from the sale of her jewellery or could have been supplemented by her cousin, James A Wickham, Thomas Sedgwick Whalley's executor, who lived until 1854. It is also possible that, until 1834, when it was sold by order of the Court of Chancery, Frances benefited from the rent of Whalley's old house in Portland Place. Clearly, had her divorce settlement of '£1,000 *per year for life*' not ceased, she would by then have been living in considerable luxury. As it was, it seems she had enough for her rent, living expenses, and one servant.

Frances died of bronchitis on 5th February, 1857, but her 1851 Will was not proved until May of that year. This contained a significant bequest to her servant, Sarah Mercer, of one year's wages plus all her clothes and linen, provided she was still in her employ at the time of her death. This seems not to have been the case, as her death certificate was witnessed with a cross by Ann

Peggs, the lodging keeper's illiterate daughter.

Frances was buried, as she had requested, in the new cemetery for the Parish of St. Peter and St Paul, just below Prior Park (Section II, A.9.10.) Her plain grave overlooks Bath and Royal Crescent and bears the inscription:

Sacred

TO THE MEMORY OF

FRANCES ELIZABETH

ONLY DAUGHTER OF THE LATE

ISAAC SAGE ESQ^R

OF THORN HILL DORSET

(FORMERLY HIGH SHERIFF

OF THAT COUNTY)

AND RELICT OF THE

REV^D. ROBERT BOYLE SULLIVAN

SHE DIED 5TH FEB 1857

AGED 86 YEARS

The grave of Frances Sullivan, née Sage.

The view from Frances' grave.

The Woodland Trust's Dolebury Warren Volunteers restoring Whalley's Lookout.

MENDIP LODGE TODAY

T HE RUINS OF Mendip Lodge (ST 467591) and its immediate surroundings are in private ownership but a well-used bridle path from Burrington Combe passes directly in front them. There is a small public car park at the bottom of the Combe on the B3143 (ST 476588), from where you can gain access to this path via Link Lane. The route is well used by visitors to the site and the nearby Dolebury Warren Iron Age hillfort (ST 450590), which was once part of the Mendip Lodge Estate.

All of Dr Whalley's estate is now within the Mendip Area of Outstanding Natural Beauty (see https://www.mendiphillsaonb.org.uk/) and is much as it was, though now owned largely by the Woodland Trust and the National Trust. The Woodland Trust's Dolebury Warren Wood contains Whalley's Lookout (ST 462592), which has been restored by the Trust's Volunteers. On clear days this vantage point still gives views of the River Severn and Welsh hills beyond.

At weekends you can usually also park in the Pear Tree industrial Estate on the A368 (ST 462596). From here an alternative access is by the Stoney Lane bridle path, which was the original drive to the house, and leads up past the stable ruins to the middle of the former estate.

In the nearby Burrington Church (ST 479593), you can still see the three memorial tablets put there by Whalley to his two wives and his first wife's first husband, John Sherwood.

From the Barley Wood Walled Garden (ST 480629), built by Henry Herbert Wills below Hannah More's original house (see https://www.walledgarden. co.uk/history), you can get some idea of how Mendip Lodge, known to her as "*Mont Blanc*", would have appeared in its heyday.

Map references are from Ordnance Survey Landranger Series Sheet 182.

APPENDICES

APPENDIX 1

THE POETRY OF THOMAS SEDGWICK WHALLEY

The following are known to have been written by TSW during his early life:

LINES ADDRESSED TO MRS WHALLEY BY HER HUSBAND
6th JANUARY 1775, THE FIRST ANNIVERSARY
OF THEIR WEDDING DAY.[314]

All hail to thee, bright ruler of the day!
May every cloud flee from thy fervent ray,
And may thy course triumphant, on this morn.
Make glad the earth, and heaven itself adorn!
Far be remov'd each sorrowing sigh, and far
Each jealous scowl and frown, each brow of care.
Nor thou, dreaded Anger, show thy scarlet face,
Nor Doubt, nor Envy, dare pollute this place.
But Mirth and Joy, and Confidence and Peace,
Be *ye* all present on a day like this!
Thus love invokes; and let it be they care,
O honour'd Hymen! To indulge the prayer;
Since on a sister day, and sister hour,
Parent of chaste desires, thy fav'ring power
First pointed out the certain path to rest,
Beguil'd my pains and calmed my tortur'd breast.
For whilom,[315] in my bosom pallid Care,
And languid Sickness, beckoned to Despair;[316]

Thought, lost in pensiveness, there held her sway,
And jealous doubtings drank my life away,
Disease triumphant totter'd in the van,
With constant Anguish, squalid, spare, and wan;
From her swoln eye still dropped the scalding tear:
Weakness was at her side, and in the rear
Sat Watchfulness and Woe; from off his stand,
The horrid dart pois'd in his wither'd hand,
In act to strike, appear'd the monster Death,
And grimly smil'd upon his prey beneath ;
But smil'd in vain: Eliza saw my need,
And new to save me with an angel's speed;
Kindly she spake; Despair conceal'd his head,
And every jealous fear and doubting fled:
Before her soothings Sorrow sank away,
And with her smiles my soul rehail'd the day.
Sick as I was, she took me to her breast,
Hush'd every sigh, and lull'd my cares to rest:
No more my mind sat brooding o'er its woe,
No more my heart all comfort would forego;
Peace once again outspread her balmy wing-,
And jocund Pleasure put forth buds of spring;
Soft Sleep his downy pinions light spread o'er
The bed, where Watchfulness had toss'd before;
And streaks of ruddy health began to break
Through the sad pale, that sallow'd my sunk cheek.
Death fled appall'd at that detested sight,
And with him fled the gloomy shades of night.
O thou! whose generous unexampled love,
Did all these evils and far more remove,
How shall my heart speak on that happy morn,
In which my blessings seem to be re-born!
From thy dear hand I date my life; from thee
My health, my peace, my independency!

o blest, most blest above the sons of men!
How shall my feelings breathe along my pen,
When my full soul its gratitude would speak,
Or tell thy virtues ? Language is too weak,
To give the one or other equal fire,
Poor is my pen, but potent my desire!
Yet to be dumb, when gratitude, when love,
When every generous impulse that can move
The throbbing heart, demand the debt of praise,
Would speak that heart still colder than my lays;
And such I know is thy humility,
That still the wish to please, will pleasure thee.
Grace, then, with smiles, this tribute of my pen,
Since love, and love alone, indites the strain !
O dearer, than the dearest terms of life,
My cheerful kind companion, friend, and wife !
Thy converse sweet this spark of life endears,
And smoothes my passage through this vale of tears.
Sweet is thy temper, sweeter far thy mind; -
To every softness, every grace inclin'd.
Complacent, humble, tender, meek, and good,
By thee no wiles were ever understood;
On thy dear brow enthron'd we always see,
Mild sense, chaste mirth, and sweet simplicity;
The govern'd passions, and the tempered smile,
And all the serpent's wit — without his guile.
Still candid, gentle, generous are thy ways,
Still kind, still prudent, past the words of praise !
Still is thy heart alive to every woe;
Still has thine eye the tear humane to flow;
Transcendent still thou art, in earthly love, '
Transcendent still thy faith in God above.
O may that Being, whose almighty will
Best pleased thou art at all times to fulfil,

Long, long, preserve thy precious life, and please

Thy health, thy joys, thy comforts to increase!

Oft may'st thou hail this blest returning morn,

And may thy virtues long the earth adorn !

And when shall come, as sure will come, the day

That frees thy spirit from surrounding clay,

Grant, O All Merciful! that from its bands,

Its passage may be easy to thy hands!

O my Eliza! best of womankind,

Pardon, if here my fond, my faltering mind,

Sickens, and weakly turns, distrest, aside

At that dread thought, which Faith and Hope deride.

And well may they deride; since souls so fine,

So free from every spot and stain as thine,

Look far beyond this world for happiness,

And in the realms above expect their bliss.

Ah ! happiest far of all, that hour of fate

When souls like thine no more their freedom wait!

Glowing with fervent love, and hope, and faith,

How will thy spirit scorn the bed of death!

How will she pant for that immortal joy,

Which ne'er will perish, and can never cloy !

How joyful will she seek her blest abode!

For pure she is, and meet to dwell with God.

VERSES ON THE COMPANY ASSEMBLED AT LANGFORD
IN THE TIME OF THE HEAVY SNOW IN 1776.[317]

Preface by Mrs Torriano, to the copy she wrote from memory in 1829, the year after Thomas' death:

"During the confinement of a large party at Langford Court for several days, in consequence of a deep snow. Miss Luders made a pen for Mr S. Whalley, and insisted on his writing her a copy of verses with it. He immediately complied, supposing the pen to speak."

> LUCRETIA has made me, and now in despite,
> She vows I shall pluck up my courage and write.
> But what can I say ? For the weather's so chill,
> That it freezes my wit, and dispirits my will.
> Say anything, nothing, as long as you write.
> Then let it be what you shall please to indite;
> And if, like yourself, I protest and declare,
> The theme will be pleasing and subject full fair.
> Pooh, pooh ! that sha'n't serve you, so e'en set about,
> The task I insist on; of what is without,
> Or within you may write, it matters not what,
> So the subject be merry and measure is pat.
> Without or within you may write; why without,
> There's nothing but snow, whisking each way about.
> In such a cold cause, it is past all dispute,
> My genius must languish, both barren and mute.
> Or, should she bring forth, you would see in a trice,
> Her offspring transformed into morsels of ice;
> And surely, my mistress, pray think me not bold,
> Can never approve of an offspring so cold.
> Within then, perforce, I my subject must find;
> I have it! 'tis suited exact to my mind.
> And first my fair maker shall furnish a theme,
> Bright as poets e'er fancied, and poets can dream;
> But a fig for their dreams; Lucretia was made

As fair as her namesake, but not half so sad.
Far distant from pouting, and making a pother,
'Bout I scarce can tell what, and calling in brother,
And father, and husband, to hear an oration
For the loss of a bauble, not worth the relation.
Then, changing her curling-tongs into a sword,
And ripping her breast for the love of her Lord,
Our Lucy[318] takes care no such slip shall undo her,
So keeps at arm's distance each buxom young wooer;
Yet smiles upon all, and, in spite of their wills,
Still murders in mirth, and subdues with her smiles.
All jaunty and tasty in manner and dress,
Full of English affection and French politesse,
Coquetting and rioting, gambling and flirting,
To the next I'll proceed, and on her drop the curtain.
Behold her co-equal in spirit and mirth,
Mad Hester,[319] whose star jigged about at her birth,
As ne'er star jigged before ; for fuller of fun,
No jolly soul ever lived under the sun.
Merry Momus stood by at the font with his darling,
And answered, as God-Dad, while Gravity, snarling,
Bit her nails out of madness; and starch Prudery
Found her gizzard in dole; such a dread enemy
She knew there was born to her squint; and, fy, fy !
But Comus, and Venus, and Euphrosyne
Joined Momus and giggled that christ'ning to see;
And swore, since their Godheads were honour'd on earth,
They ne'er were so pleased as at La Faussille's birth.
But why, in the legend of Humour and Laughter,
Should tight little Wickham[320] come hobbling' after ?
Since first, 'midst the foremost she ever will be,
In each scene of cheerfulness, frolic, and glee;
Her motions all spirit, her looks are all fun;
Those looks speak her mind, and her smart flippant tongue
To her mind or her eyes never does any wrong.
Such a trio never lived since old Momus had birth,

And with Comus and Venus enlivened the earth;
And Venus her Wickham has blest with good store
Of her charms and her graces, and, what is still more,
Tho' at variance in common, yet here Madame Die,
That Goddess so stupid, so cold, and so shy,
Relenting, has lent without scruple her aid,
With Venus, to Wickham, as wife and as maid:
As one, all her virtue and modesty gear
She lent her; as t'other,— attend and you'll hear,-—
Tho' nine times invoked, with loud squalls and a pother,
To dub Madame Dapper with title of mother,
Still, cautious has been to preserve her from harms,
And has helped to re-touch and awaken her charms.
But enough of these flippants ; a number of faces,
I yet spy around me who all demand places.
Stand by; clear the way ; first approaching, I see
A lady of merit and high quality.
Your Ladyship's humble ; how does Lady Mary? [321]
To tell you the truth, I am in a quandary,
For my fingers with cold, you may see, are quite dead,
And the frost is got into my stomach and head.
Alas! my dear lady, the matter is sad ;
But ne'er regard trifles; e'en let us be glad,
That we've got a sound roof hanging over our heads,
And can bid frost defiance with mirth and warm beds.
For while we are up, we will keep warm with laughing,
And strengthen our stomachs with eating and quaffing;
So I trust you'll do well, for a worthier dame
Never lived, I declare, in the annals of fame.
But what says fair Jenkyns to all this bad weather ?
And why are her placid brows wrinkled together ?
Indeed, Gaffer Care, you are somewhat too rude,
In a party so jovial as ours to intrude;
Tho' husbands are precious, yet husbands awhile
May be trusted to Heav'n; then let us beguile
The moments with mirth; and leave till to-morrow

Each murmuring sigh, and each symptom of sorrow,
Tho' gentle and civil, and kind and composed,
Yet still at the bottom full archly disposed.
I know the fair Jenkyns; and know sans all doubt
That a jest she can merrily bandy about;
Then clear let her brow be, and jocund her heart,
For merry we met, and in mirth let us part.
Ah, wags! t'espy you, a couple you are
Of as social spirits as e'er breathed the air.
There's Madam, the hostess of this company,
Will laugh and will jest till she scarcely can see;
And Sanford,[322] though sometimes so grave and demure,
Each frolic will mend and each joke will secure,
And add of her own, too, at pleasure (none better),
A cargo of wit, in a legible letter.
To honour, good humour, and friendship, and sense,
No pair now alive can make better pretence;
Allied as in blood, so in manners and mind
I would not disjoin, who so aptly are joined.
Behold, Madam Susan,[323] to bring up the rear,
So easy, an' please ye, so plump and sincere;
So hearty she laughs, that it does one's heart good,
And her song charms the ear, and enlivens the blood.
Pass on, my sleek Susan, and sing while ye can;
Short is life, and 'tis wise to enliven the span.
So much for the belles;' but pray where are the ' beaux?'
Oh ! not far behind them, as you may suppose;
And first (as 'tis fitting he should be) the chief,
See, bowing, the gallant Monsieur Zenovief.
What mortal can wonder we make no small fuss,
To see French politeness, engrafted on Russ;
And the Great Chamberlain of Russia's Majesty,
Appearing to grace such poor rustics as we ?
But silence there! Silence! not a word nor a squeak,
For Monsieur the Russian is going to speak.
(Votre humble, Madame, Ma'mselle Ludres; tres votre;

Madame Week, tres agreable; and you be, vous autres,
De fort jolies Anglaises.' Oh, Monsieur, Monsieur !
Your most humble servant! I cannot endure,
To be tongue-tied so vilely. Miss Luders, explain
My good wishes to Monsieur, and say with disdain,
I hold the embargo that's laid on my tongue,
Which does my esteem for the Count so much wrong-.
Lucretia interprets; and like a sly elf,
Says one word for Wicky, and two for herself;
While Monsieur, the Chamberlain, capers and chatters,
Salutes their soft hands, sighs, and ogles, and flatters;
Now talks broken English, now puts on the droll;
First plays like a monkey, then looks like a fool;
Acts the sot and the sick man, with each merry trick,
Making laughter re-echo, and gravity sick.
Agreeable, sensible, easy, polite;
The gentlemen's envy, and ladies' delight;
With the strength of a Samson, and humour of Foote;
A Mercury active, and loving to boot;
Can any one wonder, this gallant young Buss,
Has power our fair ones to charm and amuse ?
But should they at any time put on their rude airs,
Behold at his elbow, his 'aide de camp,' Luders;
Than whom upon earth, either sober or mellow,
There lives not, I swear, a more sprack little fellow.
Gay as youth can proclaim him, and jocund as day;
Full of mirth and good humour, and laughter and play;
A better companion can never be found,
To make a dull season run merrily round.
This Hetty can witness, whose lips seldom fail,
The effects of his raptures and prowess to tell;
But surely you '11 think me a fool or a sot,
Should Wickham,[324] so courteous and calm, be forgot,
Whose carriage so gentle, and manners so easy,
Can't fail, if you know whaU'5 pleasing, to please ye.
With a soul full of goodness, and kindness, and spirit,

As loved for good humour, as honoured for merit;
Sense, tempered with candour, resides in his breast,
And mirth fills his bosom, in soberness drest;
When aces and faces skim over the green,
And the conflict grows hot, betwixt knave, king and queen,
'Midst the din of the battle, who better can wield,
Of the mighty god Whist, or the sword or the shield
Yet vanquished or victor, while tumults increase,
Unmov'd he is conquer'd, and conquers in peace.
But who, says Lucretia, pray who must appear,
In so social a party, to bring up the rear ?
Can you ask, my sweet Lucy ? why, maugre all doubt,
Who conducted them in, ought to wait on them out.
Behold, then, their host[325], as alert as a bee,
As 't is proper he should be, in such company;
Tho' skinny and lank, yet he 'll laugh with the best,
And never be guilty of marring a jest.
Full of joy, hospitality, peace, and good-will,
From the crown of his head, to the tip of his heel;
And when you reflect that he's tall as a steeple,
You will fancy his portion is large, my good people;
But think once again, that he's slender as tall,
And then you may fancy his portion is small.
Be that as it may, a more social party—
More jolly, more frolicsome, free, or more hearty,
Ne'er met since Don Sancho embraced his dear Dapple,
Since Israel danced hornpipes, or Eve ate the apple.
So met and so suited, each wind may blow round;
Bain rattle, frost chill, and snow whiten the ground,

On themselves and their mirth, they repose full reliance,
And to winter, and all his assaults, bid defiance.

OCCUPANTS OF ROYAL CRESCENT, 1778[326]

1. Mr Henry Sanford – (Princess de Lamballe lived here 1786 and 1791, the Duke of York in 1796)
2. Mrs Elesha Macartney
3. Mr George Burgis
4. Mr Christopher Anstey – moved to smaller Marlborough Buildings in 1792
5. Mr John Bathoe
6. Mr Winthrop Baldwin
7. Mrs Elizabeth Tyndale – who had bought her house in 1771
8. Mr John Bennett
9. Rev Mr Whalley (The house was later renumbered as No. 20)
10. Mr John Riddle
11. Capt John Martin
12. Dr Edward Cooper
13. Mr John Charnock
14. Hon Charles Hamilton
15. Mr McGillchrist
16. Dr Claud Champion de Crespigny
17. Mrs Victory Kynaston
18. Mr Edward Hoare
19. Mr John Jefferys
20. Lady Hester Malpas
21. Lady Stepney
22. Dean of Ossory
23. Dr William Watson
24. Lady Isabella Stanley
25. Col John Stibbert
26. Mrs Mary Cunliffe
27. Lady Mary Stanley
28. Philip Thicknesse – now living here with the third Mrs Thicknesse née Ford
29. Col Champion
30. Hon Henry Greville

THE 6TH DUKE OF ARENBERG AND HIS DAUGHTER

Louis Engelbert of Arenberg (1750 –1820), nicknamed the blind duke, was the 6th Duke of Arenberg. Between 1803 and 1810, he ruled a Duchy in North-western Germany. His was one of the most prominent noble families in the Austrian Netherlands, but he had been blinded during a hunting party at the age of 24. Hill Wickham states that this was 'by the gun of the English Minister'. Unable to follow a military career, the Duke had turned to science, art and music. It was under his patronage that the first manned gas-filled balloon flight in history took off from the front lawn of Arenberg Castle on November 21st, 1783. His daughter, Pauline (1774–1810), married Count Joseph Johann von Schwarzenberg (1769–1833) but was later to die tragically trying to rescue her child from a fire. According to Hill Wickham:

> *In the summer (of 1787) they visited the Duke at his country residence. He was totally blind... but was able to enjoy riding often accompanied by Miss Sage in a gallop across his park, a servant directing the horse with a loose bridle.*

Several letters are extant, written by the young Pauline Princess D'Arenberg to Miss Sage, after her return to England (sadly only two are published in Hill Wickham Vol 2). This amiable princess married one of the Schwartzenberg family and met her death at a ball on July 16th, 1810, hosted by her brother-in-law, then Ambassador at Paris from the Court of Vienna. The Emperor, Empress and all the Court, were assembled in a temporary saloon erected for the purpose, when one of the gauze curtains took fire and, immediately communicating to all the other hangings, the whole apartment was speedily in flames. The Emperor, with great coolness, sought the Empress and led her out. Princess Pauline Schwartzenberg escaped likewise with her child; but being separated from her in the confusion, and fearing she might be still (left) behind, the princess rushed back into the saloon and was burnt to death.[327]
(See also Alison A., History of Europe during the French Revolution Volume 7, 1843, Chapter LIX.)

THE JANE AUSTEN CONNECTION

It seems highly likely that Jane (1775-1817) and her family knew of Thomas Sedgwick Whalley by reputation, even if they did not know him personally. The names of many of the people Thomas Sedgwick knew appear in Jane's correspondence.[328]

Jane's father, George Austen, and his sisters had the misfortune to lose both parents when they were very young. George was lucky to have been brought up by an aunt and sent to Tonbridge School. His sister, Philadelphia, was not so fortunate. After training as a milliner, she made her way to India to find a rich husband and the way out of her poverty, as many good looking ladies did. A companion on the boat was Margaret Maskelyne, sister of the Reverend Dr Nevil Maskelyne, fifth Astronomer Royal. She would later become a good friend, and went on to marry Robert Clive, Governor of Bengal. At about the same time, Philadelphia married Tysoe Hancock, through whom she met Warren Hastings. Hastings knew Isaac Sage for, indeed, it was Hastings who had recommended a relation of Lord Apsley to him while he was Governor of Patna.[329] In 1761, Philadelphia gave birth to her only child, Elizabeth; Warren Hastings was rumoured to have been the father, and certainly he supported the child very generously. The experiences of Philadelphia and her daughter would later become woven into Jane's novels.

The Reverend George Austen (1731–1805) was married at Walcot in Bath, in 1764, and would later be buried there. From 1773 onward, the Rev Austen took in a series of well-connected boys as pupils to supplement the family income at the Steventon village rectory. Jane's mother Cassandra, (née Leigh 1739-1827), was a contemporary of Thomas Sedgwick Whalley, and spent her youth in Bath, and so knew it well. Jane Austen's aunt (her mother's elder sister), Jane Leigh, and her husband, Rev Dr Edward Cooper, lived in Royal Crescent and Ison records them as living only four doors away from the Whalleys.[330] The Reverend Cooper, like Thomas Sedgwick, was a Prebend of Wells Cathedral, though senior to him, and both became Doctors of Divinity; Jane's mother and Jane Cooper (née Leigh) seem to have been in frequent correspondence.

Mrs Whalley claimed that her father, Edward Jones, had some intimacy with (the 1st) Lord Portsmouth and his family.[331] Some years later, the Rev George Austen accepted the young Lord Lymington (1767-1853) to his school in early 1773,[332] but he was removed on the grounds of health in December of that year.[333] Nonetheless, the Austen family maintained some contact with the 2nd Lord Portsmouth.

Jane Austen's uncle, her mother's elder brother James Leigh Perrot (1735-1812), and his wife Jane Cholmeley (1744-1836), were a wealthy couple who were always referred to in Jane's letters as 'my uncle and my aunt'. The Leigh Perrots soon developed the habit of spending half the year on their estate in Berkshire and the other half in Bath at No 1 Paragon Buildings.[334] This is precisely what the Whalley's were accustomed to doing, alternating between Mendip Lodge in Upper Langford and Royal Crescent in Bath.

Jane probably knew Fanny Burney personally because Jane's godfather, Reverend Samuel Cooke, was a close friend of the Burneys. Jane admired Fanny Burney's first novel '*Evelina*' and was one of the subscribers to her third novel '*Camilla*', published in 1796. Fanny Burney had been a guest of the Whalley's in Bath in 1780, and a number of their friends were also subscribers to the novel (Hannah More, Humphrey Repton, Rev William Mason, and Mrs Porteus). Mrs Piozzi and her daughters subscribed 12 copies between them. Thomas Sedgwick himself did not subscribe, but at the time his niece Frances was going through her divorce and perhaps he had no desire to read such things.

Jane Austen's first novel '*Lady Susan*' copied the epistolary style of Fanny Burney's '*Evelina*'. It was probably written in 1793-4, though the only known manuscript is a copy dated 1805.[335] The locations of "Langford" and "Churchill" as the addresses of the two main characters, Lady Susan and Mrs Vernon, are intriguing. By this time, Thomas Sedgwick Whalley had completed the building of his cottage at Langford, later to become known as Mendip Lodge, and was entertaining the great and good there during the summer months. He was still the owner of Langford Court, although this was let in 1794 to his good friend Henry Bosanquet, who had married Christopher Anstey's daughter Caroline in 1790.[336]

There are no surviving letters of Jane Austen before 1796, and the date of her first visit to Bath was in November/ December 1797, when the 22-year-old stayed with the Leigh Perrots in Paragon Buildings. The Whalleys were certainly in Bath at this time.[337] Jane and her family were again in Bath, from 17th May, 1799, until June 22nd, 1799, when they rented 13 Queen Square. Thomas, though, was in London awaiting the production of his play 'The Castle of Montval' at Drury Lane.

Alethea Bigg was a long-standing friend from Austen's childhood at Steventon. Jane had attended the Bigg's Manydown Ball, where Catherine Bigg was her favourite partner when men were in short supply.[338] Their sister Elizabeth married the Reverend William Heathcote (1772-1802), a Prebendary of Winchester, who was a relative of Thomas Sedgwick's second wife, Augusta Heathcote, of Devizes. Elizabeth Heathcote's name appears in many of Jane's letters but there is no evidence that they ever had any connection with the Devizes branch of the Heathcote family. William died shortly before Augusta, in 1802, whereupon Elizabeth returned to Manydown to become a neighbour of Jane; she had copies of all Jane's books.

It is quite probable that Thomas Sedgwick knew the Reverend Gilbert Heathcote MA Oxon (1765-1829).[339] Gilbert was later Archdeacon of Winchester and eventually became Treasurer of Wells in 1814, under the patronage of Bishop Richard Beadon, who was Thomas Sedgwick's cousin. The Reverend Gilbert married Maria Lyell but it is not clear if she was related to the Lyells in Jane's correspondence.

It was in 'Northanger Abbey', written in 1798/9 but not published until after Jane's death in 1817, that the Master of Ceremonies of the Lower Rooms, James King, introduced Catherine to the book's hero, Henry Tilney. James King was the Master of Ceremonies of the Lower Rooms at the time of Jane's visit in 1797, and is one of the few living people to be mentioned in one of her novels. One wonders if it is his daughter Miss King to whom Miss Weston refers to as leading Frances Sage astray in May 1789? It is perhaps of relevance that Miss Weston's husband, Mr Pennington, became the Master of Ceremonies at Hotwells, Bristol, in 1785.

REFERENCES

JCTSW = Wickham, H.D., *Journals and correspondence of Thomas Sedgwick Whalley DD.*, Richard Bentley, London, 1863, 2 vols.

TIL = Bloom, E.A., Bloom, L.D., *The Piozzi Letters* Vols I-VI. Associate Universities Presses, London, 1999.

TPL = Knapp, O.G., *The intimate letters of Hester Piozzi and Penelope Pennington 1788-1821*, John Lane, The Bodley Head, London, 1913.

1   JCTSW I p.6
2   *Clergy of the Church of England Database,* (http://www.theclergydatabase.org.uk/jsp/persons/index.jsp)
3   Venn, J.A., Alumni Cantabrigienses. Part II volume VI, Cambridge University Press, Cambridge, 1954.
4   See Gillard D, *Education in England: a brief history* 2011 (http://www.educationengland.org.uk/history)
5   Another ancestor, Thomas Whalley (died 1637), had donated three volumes of Boissard's Topographia Romana Urbis (1597) to the college library which are still there today. The books' previous owner had been King James I but the reason for their presentation to Thomas' namesake is unknown.
6   Ingamells J, *A dictionary of British and Irish travellers in Italy* 1701-1800, Yale University Press, Newhaven, 1997.
7   Lysons, D., *The Environs of London*: Vol. 3 - County of Middlesex, 1795, pp.391-403
8   National Archives. *Records of the East India College*, 1762. IRO /J/1/4/380-383
9   Williams, C., *The Nabobs of Berkshire*, Goosecroft Publications, Purley on Thames, Berkshire, 2010, p.112
10 JCTSW I p.8
11 Williams, C., *The Nabobs of Berkshire*, Goosecroft Publications, Purley on Thames, Berkshire, 2010, p.191
12 JCTSW, I p.152
13 McCormack, R., *Leisured Women and the English Spa Town in the Long Eighteenth Century: A Case Study of Bath and Tunbridge Wells*. PhD Thesis,University of Aberystwyth, 2015. Chapter 2
14 JCTSW I p.6
15 There is more than one account of Joseph appearing in court as an expert witness for the Crown when silver coinage had been tampered with by "clipping"
16 Clergy of the Church of England Database http://www.theclergydatabase.org.uk/ Entry 40820
17 Although graduate of Caius Keene became a Fellow of Peterhouse and obtained his Doctorate there in the time of Whalley's father
18 JCTSW I p.3
19 ibid I pp.263-4
20 ibid II p.503
21 ibid I p.272
22 In fact she would not do so for another three years
23 JCTSW I p.273
24 ibid I p.274
25 ibid I pp.269-71
26 Rumbold had been Clive's aide de camp at the Battle of Plassey and the following year would be returned as MP for the rotten borough of Shaftesbury
27 JCTSW I p.279
28 ibid I p.281
29 ibid I pp.270-1
30 As the Jones family were descended from Cadwallader Jones (c1632-c1692), which had inherited property in Wales as well as America, this might explain how Elizabeth Sherwood had come to know George Warrington and his circle in Wrexham
31 JCTSW I pp.278-9
32 William, C., *The Nabobs of Wiltshire*, Goosecroft Publications, Purley on Thames, Berkshire, 2010, pp.338-341

33   JCTSW I p.280

34   ibid I p.231

35   Courtney,W.P., *Whalley, Thomas Sedgwick (1746–1828)*, revised. Rebecca Mills, Oxford Dictionary of National Biography, Oxford University Press, 2004

36   *Theatre Royal Bath A calendar of performances at the Orchard Street Theatre 1750-1805*, (Hare, A., Ed), Kingsmead Press, Bath, 1977, p.29

37   JCTSW I p.4

38   ibid I pp.246-252

39   Though his father wrote poetry he had died before Thomas was two-years-old

40   Marsden-Smedley, C., *Burrington Church and Village – a short history*, Burrington, 1991, p.21

41   JCTSW I p.4

42   Gosse, P., *Dr Viper, the querulous life of Philip Thicknesse*, Cassell and Company Ltd, London, 1952

43   Lowndes, W., *The Royal Crescent in Bath*, Redcliffe Press Ltd., Bristol, 1981, p.43

44   Ison, W., *The Georgian Buildings of Bath 1730-1830*, Kingsmead Press, 1980

45   Lowndes, W., *The Royal Crescent in Bath*, Redcliffe Press Ltd., Bristol, 1981, p.48

46   Rizzo, B., *Early Journals and Letters of Fanny Burney. Volume IV The Streatham Years*, Part II, 1780-1781, Oxford University Press, 2003, pp.126-9

47   The New Bath Guide gained him praise at the time from those not noted for such generosity, including Hugh Walpole and Thomas Gray

48   ibid I pp.311-2

49   It is curious that although Hill Wickham refers to him as Mr Anstey Calvert, Thomas Sedgwick only ever calls him Arthur Anstey

50   Bath Chronicle and Weekly Gazette, May 6th, 1790

51   Sturge, M., *MrsMiller* Recorded lecture given to the Bath Literary and Scientific Institution 23 Nov 2009. (http://www.bath.ac.uk/lmf/fileinfo/37757 accessed 31/03/2015)

52   JCTSW I p.315

53   JCTSW I p.6

54   *Theatre Royal Bath A calendar of performances at the Orchard Street Theatre 1750-1805*, (Hare, A., ed), Kingsmead Press, Bath, 1977, p.63

55   JCTSW I pp.370-1

56   ibid I pp.338-9

57   See Stephens, C.D., *The Reverend Dr Thomas Sedgwick Whalley and the Queen of Bath.*

  Candy Jar Books, Cardiff, 2014, pp.37-8

58   JCTSW I p.22

59   ibid II p.109

60   ibid II pp.119-120

61   ibid II p.121

62   ibid I p.273

63   ibid I p.278

64   Dutt, G.N., *History of the Hutwa Raj, Calcutta*, 1904, p.209

65   Letter from Gregorious Herklots to Isaac Sage 30th August, 1775, and Sage's reply, 31st August, 1775. Enclosures to memoir of outgoing Dutch Director Bacheracht to his successor, HRB 253 (*unfoliated*) Archives and Records Association

66   JCTSW I pp.282-3

67   ibid I p.286

68   See http://freepages.genealogy.rootsweb.ancestry.com/~dutillieul/ZOtherPapers/NewS&WJ2Oct1775.html

69   This would later be converted into living rooms by the Revd W Boucher

70   JCTSW I p.6

71   ibid I p.288

72   ibid I p.284

73   ibid I pp.292-3

74   ibid I pp.305-8

75   William, C., *The Nabobs of Wiltshire*. Goosecroft Publications, Purley on Thmas, Berkshire, 2010, p.113

76   JCTSW I p.6

77   Jewers, A.J., *Wells Cathedral: its monumental inscriptions and heraldry*, Mitchell and Hughes, London, 1892, pp.171-3

78   JCTSW I p.6

79   *Church of England Parish Registers 1538-1812*, London Metropolitan Archives, London

80   Bannerman, W.B., *The Parish Registers of Gatton and of Sanderstead in Surrey*, The Surrey Parish Register Society, 1908

81   Boswell, E., *The civil division of the county of Dorset*, Crutwell, Sherborne, 1795

82   JCTSW I p.384

83   Fryer J., Langford Court. In *Every House tells a story*, Langford History Group, Langford, 2006, p.28

84   The Gunnings would continue to live there until 1788

85   Lowndes, W., *The Royal Crescent in Bath*, Redcliffe Press, Bristol, 1981, p.50

86   JCTSW I pp.15-6

87   ibid I pp.169-230

88   ibid I p.16

89   This seems to have been something of

a habit of the French Court. Some years earlier, Louis XV had referred to the young Sir William Draper as 'le beau garcon anglias'. See Dreaper, J., *Bristol's forgotten victor*. Bristol Branch of the Historical Association, Bristol, 1998, p7

90 JCTSW I pp.404-8

91 Lowndes, W., *The Royal Crescent in Bath*, Redcliffe Press, Bristol, 1981, p.50

92 JCTSW I p.404

93 ibid I p.422

94 ibid I p.420

95 ibid I p.430

96 ibid I p.431

97 ibid I p.463 (Footnote)

98 ibid II p.41

99 Burchell, J., *Polite or commercial concerts? Concert management and orchestral repertoire in Edinburgh, Bath, Oxford, Manchester and Newcastle 1730-1799* Garland, New York, 1996. p.160

100 JCTSW I p.408

101 ibid I p.440

102 ibid I p.472

103 ibid I p.477

104 ibid II pp.79-80 (& footnote)

105 TPL I p.195

106 JCTSW I p.227

107 ibid I p.228

108 ibid II p.15

109 ibid II p.6 (Footnote)

110 ibid I p.408

111 Austen, J Mansfield Park, 1814

112 JCTSW II p.14

113 ibid II pp.23-4

114 Somerset Heritage Centre,Taunton, Somerset. Reference DD/X/MT/5

115 He would be married to Caroline Anstey in 1790, Thomas Sedgwick Whalley performing the ceremony

116 JCTSW I p.188

117 ibid II p.23

118 *Edmund Rack's Survey of Somerset*, McDermott, M and Berry, S (Eds), Somerset Archaeological Society 2009, p.57

119 *Letters of Anna Seward, Written Between the Years 1784 and 1807*, (Constable, A., Ed), Vol 2, George Ramsay and Co., Edinburgh, 1811, p.169

120 Somers, B.E., *Pedigree of the family of Somers of Mendip Lodge – Somerset*, 1916, p.6 (Somerset Heritage Trust, Local Studies Catalogue. Ref GRN 0328115)

121 By this time her eldest son, Edward, had been lost at sea.

122 TPL II p.124 (Note 9)

123 JCTSW II p.287

124 *Letters of Anna Seward, Written Between the Years 1784 and 1807*, (Constable, A., Ed), *Vol III*, George Ramsay and Co., Edinburgh, 1811, pp.96-101

125 JCTSW II p.197 (Footnote)

126 *Letters of Anna Seward, Written Between the Years 1784 and 1807* (Constable, A., Ed), *Vol VI*, George Ramsay and Co Edinburgh, 1811, pp.202-5

127 ibid Vol III, p.107

128 ibid Vol III pp.202-205

129 De Quincey, T., *The Works of Thomas De Quincey*, (North, J., Ed), Vol. 11, Articles from Taits Magazine and Blackwoods Magazine 1838-41, Pickering and Chatto, London, 2003, pp.239-240

130 Public Act 33 George III c165, 1793. Records of the House of Lords. HL/PO/PU/1/1793/33G3n168

131 Tate, W.E., *Somerset Enclosure Acts and Awards*. Somerset Archaeological and Natural History Society, 1948

132 Bilingsley, J., *General view of the agriculture in the county of Somerset*. Board of Agriculture, London 1794, pp.34-43

133 *Letters of Anna Seward, Written Between the Years 1784 and 1807*, (Constable, A., Ed), *Vol. IV*, George Ramsay and Co, Edinburgh, 1811, p.43

134 JCTSW II p.41

135 *Letters of Anna Seward, Written Between the Years 1784 and 1807*, (Constable, A., Ed), *Vol. III*, George Ramsay and Co Edinburgh, 1811, p.379

136 Lowndes, W., *The Royal Crescent in Bath*. The Redcliffe Press, Bristol, 1981. p.50

137 White, B., *Who was the Queen of Bath?* in Bath History XII, Bath Preservation Trust, Bath, 2011

138 JCTSW II p.33

139 It has also been suggested that the tall gentleman with the white hair is Thomas Sedgwick himself

140 *Letters of Anna Seward, Written Between the Years 1784 and 1807*, (Constable, A., Ed.), *Vol. I*, George Ramsay and Co., Edinburgh, 1811, p.128

141 ibid Vol III pp.172-3

142 ibid Vol III p.204

143 Sarah Anne, the youngest daughter of Sir Riggs Falkiner, first Baronet of Anne Mount,

County Cork

144 *Alumni Dublinenses*, (Burtchaell G, Sadleir T, Eds.), London, 1924

145 *An Act to dissolve the Marriage of William Mullins and Frances Elizabeth Sage*. 36 Geo III 1796/6

146 Morning Post and Advertiser, 10th January 1791

147 Ylivouri, S., *Women and politeness in the 18th century*. Routledge, New York, 2019

148 Porter, R., *English Society in the 18th century*, Penguin Books, London, 1982, p.307

149 *Letters of Anna Seward, Written Between the Years 1784 and 1807*, (Constable, A., Ed.), Vol. IV,. George Ramsay and Co Edinburgh, 1811, p.44

150 White, G.H,. Lea, R.S., *The Complete Peerage, or a history of the House of Lords and all its members from the earliest times*, St. Catherine Press, London, 1959; XII, pp.238-241

151 Greenwoolers, C., Witness statement., Consistory Court of London, 2nd June 1795. Parliamentary Archives reference HL/PO/PB/1/1796/36G3n116

152 *Letters of Anna Seward, Written Between the Years 1784 and 1807*, (Constable, A., Ed.), Vol. III,. George Ramsay and Co Edinburgh, 1811, p.47

153 Daxon, J., Witness Statement, Consistory Court of London, 2nd June 1795. Parliamentary Archives reference HL/PO/PB/1/1796/36G3n116

154 Porter, R., English Society in the 18th century. Penguin Books, London, 1982, pp.27-8

155 Vickery, A., *The gentleman's daughter – womens' lives in Georgian England*, Yale University Press, London, 2003. p.160

156 JCTSW II p.414

157 At the end of his life, Thomas Sedgwick was still trying to recover a loan which he had made to William of £500, on which even the interest had not been paid (Undated letter from Thomas Sedgwick Whalley to William Bromley, of Grays Inn Square, London, 1827, now in possession of the author)

158 JCTSW II p.90

159 ibid II p.85

160 There is no evidence that he did so but, in October, 1803, a William Mullins (Gent) enrolled as an Ensign in the first East Somerset Regiment

161 *Letters of Anna Seward, Written Between the Years 1784 and 1807*, (Constable, A., Ed.), Vol.

IV, George Ramsay and Co., Edinburgh, 1811, pp.42-4

162 Deposition by Maria Brazier, 26th May, 1795. Parliamentary Archives reference HL/PO/PB/1/1796/36G3n116

163 Woolfram, S., *Divorce in England 1700 – 1857*. Oxford Journal of Legal Studies 1985; 5: 162

164 These were provided by Mary Bennet (Chambermaid), Maria Brazier (Ladies Maid), John Constable (Inn Keeper), Frances Glaysher (Chamber maid), Patrick Kenny (Sedan Chairman), Matthews Mullins (Groom), Joseph Randall (Postboy), James Sage (Valet)

165 Woolfram, S., *Divorce in England 1700 – 1857*. Oxford Journal of Legal Studies 1985; 5: 155-185

166 *The Bath Gazette and Weekly Advertiser*, July 23rd 1795, p.2

167 *The Ipswich Journal*, July 25th 1795, p.2

168 *The Times*, July 28th 1795, p.1

169 A senior court of common law at that time

170 Private Act George III c 47. Records of the House of Lords. HL/PO/PB/1/1796/36G3n116

171 Smith, S.D., *Slavery family and gentry in the British Atlantic*, Cambridge University Press, Cambridge, 2006

172 *Bath Chronicle*, February 26th, 1784

173 Holborne Museum, Bath. http://www.holborne.org/muse/search/item.cfm?MuseumNumber=2008.1 [accessed 24/09/2013]

174 Holborne Museum of Art Annual Report, Bath, 2007, p.9

175 His son, Thomas, was born the same year, which strongly suggests that William was not going to be caught out again by marrying a barren wife

176 Letter from Thomas Sedgwick Whalley to Wm Bromley, April, 1827, now in the author's possession

177 JCTSW II p.413

178 ibid II p.412

179 Burke, Sir B., *A genealogical and heraldic history of the commoners of Great Britain and Ireland*, 1895, p.345

180 Smith, H.S., *The Parliaments of England 1715-1847*, 2nd Ed., (Craig, F., Ed.), Parliamentary Reference Publications, Chichester, 1973

181 TIL p.129

182 *Letters of Anna Seward, Written Between the Years 1784 and 1807*, (Constable, A., Ed.), Vol IV, George Ramsay and Co., Edinburgh, 1811, p.44

183   ibid p.127

184   TPL II p.239

185   *Letter from Penelope Pennington to Mrs Piozzi, 27th March, 1795*, The John Rylands Library, University of Manchester, 567.57

186   Mrs Piozzi states that it was only £500 and this increased by the generosity of her former husband. See TPL II p.340 note 1

187   London England Banns, 1754-1921.

188   Bigwood, R., *Lawrence families of the Builth Wells and Llanelwedd area in the 18th and 19th centuries,* Radnorshire Society Transactions, 1989, 59: 96-99

189   *St James Winscombe Banns 1754-1811,* Weston-super-Mare Family History Society, 2004

190   Dr Beadon was, in turn, Archdeacon of London (1775); Master of Jesus College Cambridge (1781); Bishop of Gloucester (1798); and in 1802, was translated to the diocese of Bath and Wells, over which he presided for 22 years

191   JCTSW II p.35 (Footnote)

192   *Alumni Dublinenses,* (Burtchaell, G., Sadlier, T., Eds.), London, 1924

193   Todd, J. H., *Catalogue of Graduates of Dublin University who have proceeded to Degrees in the University of Dublin*, Hodges Smith and Foster, Dublin, 1868

194   Brady, W.M., *The Clerical and Parochial Records of Cloyne, Cork and Ross*, Alexander Thom, Dublin, 1863, Vol. 3, p.254

195   *Boyle Farm* 4th Ed., S and R Bentley, London 1828

196   JCTSW I p.38

197   *Letters of Anna Seward, Written Between the Years 1784 and 1807*, (Constable, A., Ed.), *Vol. IV*, George Ramsay and Co. Edinburgh, 1811, p.43-4; p.50

198   ibid V pp.111-2

199   ibid III pp.42-5

200   *Letters of Anna Seward, Written Between the Years 1784 and 1807*, (Constable, A., Ed.), *Vol. VI*, George Ramsay and Co. Edinburgh, 1811, p.395

201   TIL p.171

202   TPL III p.115

203   JCTSW II p.48

204   ibid I p.24

205   London Gazette, 1803, Issue 15637 Oct. 26th, p.1498

206   *Diocese of Bath and Wells presentation papers*, Somerset Heritage Centre, Taunton, Somerset, Ref D/D/Bp/148-154.

207   JCTSW II.p.473

208   The first five children of John and Frances Stafford were born in Winscombe. The first daughter, born in 1812, was named Thomasina after her grandmother. Four other children were born there between 1814 and 1820

209   A Mr Torriano also attended Thomas Sedgwick Whalley's funeral in La Fléche. He is described by Hill Wickham as being *'the son of one of his oldest and most intimate friends'* (JCTSW I p.38). In fact, this was probably a grandson of Charles Stafford, (1716-1791) born in Wells and who died in Bath, but he does not seem to be mentioned in any letter of the two Hill Wickham volumes. A Major Torriano, perhaps his son, is described as having been killed at Toulon when it was taken by Napoleon in 1793 (JCTSW I p.247)

210   Constable A (Ed), *Letters of Anna Seward, Written Between the Years 1784 and 1807,*. Vol. II, George Ramsay and Co., Edinburgh, 1811, p.169

211   ibid Vol II p.301

212   JCTSW I p.31

213   ibid I pp.231-4

214   ibid II p.242

215   TPL III p.341 Note 10. Sadly no source to the letter referred to is given

216   JCTSW II p.220

217   See Stephens, C.D., *The Reverend Dr Thomas Sedgwick Whalley and the Queen of Bath.* Candy Jar Books, Cardiff, 2014 Chapter 9: The Blagdon Controversy

218   Constable A (Ed), *Letters of Anna Seward, Written Between the Years 1784 and 1807 Vol. V*, George Ramsay and Co., Edinburgh, 1811, p.426

219   ibid Vol IV, p.115

220   The London Magazine and Monthly Chronologer, Volume 9, 1740. p 506

221   JCTSW I pp.31-2

222   Heathcote, D.E., *An account of some of the families bearing the name Heathcote which have descended out of the County of Derbyshire.* Warren and Sons Ltd., Winchester, 1899, p.69

223   JCTSW II p.231

224   ibid II p.245

225   ibid II pp.249-50

226   ibid II p.278

227   Lucas, E.V., *A Swan and her friends*, Methuen and Co, London, 1900, p.201

228   JCTSW I p.32

229 ibid II pp.307-9

230 ibid I p.33

231 ibid II pp.317-8

232 ibid II p.323

233 ibid II p.322

234 Whalley T.S., *Kenneth and Fenella – a legendary tale*. Hatchard J, London, 1809

235 JCTSW I p.33

236 ibid II p.314

237 ibid II p.223

238 ibid II p.228

239 ibid II p.332

240 TPL V p.154

241 JCTSW I p.33

242 Private Act, 16 George III, c. 85 HL/PO/PB/1/1776/16G3n147

243 Rauser, A.F., *Caricature unmasked: irony, authenticity and individualism in 18th century prints*, Associated Universities Presses, New Jersey, 2008

244 Captain Able Rouse Dottin was later also based here – see Chapter 7

245 ibid I p.33

246 TPL V p.154

247 ibid V p.155

248 De Quincey, T., *The works of Thomas de Quincey Vol 11: Articles from Taits Magazine*,(North, J. Ed.), Pickering and Chatto, London, 2003, p.239

249 JCTSW II p.377 (Footnote)

250 JCTSW I p.34

251 JCTSW II p.372

252 TPL V p.283 (Footnote 1)

253 The Peace of Paris was signed in June, 1815, and many now returned to the continent.

254 TPL V p.282

255 JCTSW II pp.384-5

256 ibid pp.390-2. It is of significance that Hannah More refers to her as 'your fille' and it is true Frances had been like a daughter to him for many years though never referred to like this anywhere else

257 ibid II p.393

258 This was John Clarke. See Stephens, C.D., *The Reverend Dr Thomas Sedgwick Whalley and the Queen of Bath*. Candy Jar Books, Cardiff, 2014 Appendix 5, *The Will of Thomas Sedgwick Whalley*

259 JCTSW II pp.401-3

260 JCTSW II pp.412-3

261 This seems to reflect the practice of including a mother's surname as part of a child's name, but a widow including a previous husband's name after a second marriage does not seem to have been commonplace

262 TPL V p.348

263 ibid I p.40

264 TPL VI pp.176-7

265 ibid p.192

266 JCTSW II p.442

267 There is a suggestion that Whalley may have also rented a house in Connaught Terrace, Paddington, at this time. See Paddington Tyburnia in *A History of the County of Middlesex* Elrington, C.R.(Ed) Vol 9 (1989) pp.190-198

268 JCTSW I p.36

269 TIL p.285

270 This was a nephew by her marriage to her second husband. He had been so named in the hope that Mrs Piozzi would support her husband's brother's family. In the end JSPS received her house, Brynbella, along with the rest of Mrs Piozzi's estates in Flint, Denbigh and Caernarvonshire, thus becoming one of the foremost landowners in Wales

271 TIL p.279

272 JCTSW I p.36

273 ibid p.470 and footnote

274 ibid I p.36

275 Bath Chronicle and Weekly Gazette, August 13th, 1829

276 Bath Chronicle and Weekly Gazette, 19th April, 1832

277 Bath Chronicle and Weekly Gazette, 20th September, 1832

278 JCTSW I p.470

279 The house was eventually sold in February, 1834, after a Decree of the Court of Chancery, following an action taken by Augusta Edgell against Thomas' Executor, James Wickham

280 JCTSW II p.462

281 JCTSW II p.462 (Footnote)

282 Papers of the late Commander M.Lawder.. Somerset Heritage Centre, Taunton. Unlisted collection, ref A/CHZ Acc M/1386. Box 8 Deeds 4 p.583 and Deeds 2 p.268

283 Arthur Anstey (Calvert) was an attorney and son of Christopher Anstey, author of the New Bath Guide

284 JCTSW II p.476

285 Nor have I been able to discover anything else about his life after he left the curacy of Bradford-on-Avon - CDS

286 *Ruin in the Mendips - the end of an eighteenth century castle in the air*, The Times, October

9th, 1958, p.12

287 Coyshe, A.W., Mason, E.J., Waite, V. *The Mendips*, Robert Hale Ltd, London, 1954, p.130

288 London Gazette, 9th December, 1822.

289 At the end of 1819 he transferred from Southampton to Warminster - probably to Lord Weymouth's Grammar School, established 1707, whose pupils had included Thomas Arnold, later Head Master of Rugby, and Samuel Squire, Bishop of St Davids, who might well have been related to Thomas Sedgwick on his mother's side

290 JCTSW I p.36

291 ibid II p.487

292 ibid II p.493

293 ibid II p.496

294 ibid I p.37

295 Thompson,H., *The life of Hannah More with notices of her sisters*. W. Blackwood and Sons, Edinburgh, 1838

296 Scott, A., *Hannah More the first Victorian*. Oxford University Press, Oxford, 2003

297 Hopkins,M.A., *Hannah More and her circle*. Longmans, London, 1947

298 *Registers of the Bishops of Bath and Wells*, Somerset Heritage Centre, Taunton, Somerset Ref D/D/B Reg 34 f.31v

299 Letter dated April 27th, 1828, addressed to Mr Bromley, of Gray's Inn Square, London, now in the possession of the author

300 JCTSW II p.504

301 ibid II p.505

302 Ibid II pp.506-7

303 The Will of Thomas Sedgwick Whalley, June 24th, 1824. Public Record Office National Archive Catalogue Ref. Prob.11/1752.Image Ref 148

304 Hill Wickham says the 3rd but the death certificate says the 4th at 'trois heures du soir'

305 JCTSW I p.38

306 Coysh, A.W., Mason, E.J., Waite. V., *The Mendips*, Robert Hale Ltd, London, 1954, p.132

307 Bath Chronicle, 15th September, 1828

308 Rutter,J.,*Delineations of the North Western Division of the County of Somerset and of its antediluvian Bone Caverns,*.Longman Rees and Co., London, 1829, pp.112-3

309 Lowndes, W., *They came to Bath*, Redcliffe Press, Bristol, 1982, p.90

310 Tilley, C., *The political process in revolutionary France 1830–1832*, University of Michigan, 1973

311 For a full account of these events see Latimer E.W., *France in the 19th Century 1830-1890*, Bibliobazaar Books, Charleston, 2006

312 Lowndes, W., *The Royal Crescent in Bath*. Redcliffe Press, Bristol, 1981, pp.81-2

313 Egan, P., *Walks through Bath.*,Meyler and Son, Bath, 1819. pp.139-40

314 JCTSW I pp.231-4

315 = formerly

316 Hill Wickham says this refers to TSW's illness occasioned by a fall from his horse causing concussion of the brain

317 JCTSW I pp.246-52

318 Mrs G. Anstey

319 Miss LaFaussille, afterwards married to Major Torriano, killed at Toulon, when retaken by Bonaparte, 1793

320 His sister Mary, born 1742, ob. 1817

321 Hill Wickham's footnote just says 'Knollis' but this seems to mean Lady Mary Knollis (Knollys)

322 Mrs Rodd

323 His sister Mrs Crane

324 Mr Wickham, of Frome, who married Dr Whalley's sister, Mary. He died in 1791

325 Thomas Sedgwick Whalley himself

326 Ison, W., *The Georgian Buildings of Bath 1730-1830*, Kingsmead Press, 1980

327 JCTSW I p.20

328 *Jane Austen's Letters* LeFaye, D., (Ed). Oxford University Press, 3rd Ed.,Oxford, 1995

329 JCTSW I p.309

330 Ison W. *The Georgian buildings of Bath*. Colin Johnson, 1990

331 JCTSW I p.431

332 *The Austen papers* R.A Austen-Leigh (Ed). Spottiswoode, Ballantyne and Co. Ltd., Colchester, 1942 .p.29

333 He was later declared insane

334 Later, Thomas' niece Frances Sullivan would come to live at No2 Paragon Buildings (see chapter 10)

335 Southam BC., *Jane Austen's Literary Manuscripts*, Clarendon Press, Oxford, 1964. Chapter 3

336 Bath Chronicle and Weekly Gazette. Tuesday 6th May, 1790

337 JCTSW I p.108

338 Byrne P. *The real Jane Austen*. Harper Press London, 2013. p.94

339 No less than 32 Heathcotes graduated from Oxford and 16 of these held holy orders

PICTURE CREDITS

SRO = Somerset Record Office

JCTSW = from Hill Wickham Journals and Correspondence of Thomas Sedgwick Whalley 1863

Front cover Print in possession of the author; Inset: JCTSW Vol 1

Back cover Copyright Bath in Time – Bath Reference library with kind permission

Page 5 Author's own collection

Page 10 Author's own collection

Page 13 JCTSW Vol 1

Page 18 By kind permission of the Trustees of the British Museum

Page 19 Author's own collection

Page 23 London Metropolitan Archives, City of London P89/MRY1/166

Page 27 Authors own collection

Page 31 Author's own collection

Page 32 Author's own collection

Page 33 From Lady Anna Riggs Miller *Poetical Amusements at a Villa near Bath*. Volume 1 2nd Ed London, 1776

Page 36 Author's own collection, by kind permission of the Chapter of Wells Cathedral

Page 37 Author's own collection – from the on line Estate agents details from 10 years ago

Page 43 Top image Author's own collection by kind permission of the Chapter of Wells Cathedral

Lower Transcribed by the author from the above

Page 46 Drawn by the author

Page 55 SRO Reference DD\OB\15 by kind permission

Page 56 Print in possession of the author

Page 59 Postcards from Mr Frank Coker's Collection by kind permission

Page 60 Photo by kind permission of Mr Pat Wilson

Pages 63-65 SRO Reference DD\OB\15 and DD\X/MT/5 by kind permission

Page 67 Redrawn and modified by the author

from *Billingsley J General view of the Agriculture of Somerset 2nd Ed 1798*

Page 68 Drawn by the author

Page 71 Copyright Bath in Time – Bath Reference library with kind permission

Page 74 Lefthand: from JCTSW Vol 1; Right hand Oil painting in possession of the author

Page 80 Painting by William Mulready RA "The Mall Kensington Gravel Pits"(1812) by kind permission of the V&A

Page 83 National Portrait Gallery with kind permission

Page 87 London Metropolitan Archives, City of London P89/MRY1/176

Page 92 Image taken by the author

Page 96 Taken by the author with kind permission of the Rev. Nicholas Maddock

Page 98 Reproduced with kind permission of The Institute of Heraldic and Genealogical Studies, www.ihgs.ac.uk

Page 102 Taken by the author with kind permission of the Rev. Nicholas Maddock

Page 106 By kind permission of Dr Moira Bonnimgton

Page 108 National Portrait Gallery with kind permission

Page 115 Image taken by the author

Page 122 Images taken and modified by the author

Page 125 Postcard in possession of the author

Page 127 Image kindly taken by Mme Monique Massée forwarded to the author

Page128 Image kindly taken by Mme Monique Massée forwarded to the author

Page 132 Image taken by the author

Page 133 Image taken by the author

Page 134 Image taken by the author

INDEX